STAND MIXER
RECIPES FOR BEGINNERS

Simple and Delicious Recipes for Your Stand Mixer

NATASHA MILLER

CONTENTS

Introduction

W hether you're making a summery fruit dessert or want some fluffy rolls to supplement your next dinner party menu, there's a lot you can do with a stand mixer.

It can do everything from mixing up cakes and cookies to creating perfectly aerated whipped cream. This versatile device can even be used for savory recipes, like mashed potatoes, dips and home-baked bread. There's no shortage of ways to use this clever appliance...provided you have a few handy recipes at the ready, that is. And that's this book comes in.

Thanks to that most beloved of kitchen gadgets, we can whisk, whip, knead and combine an array of ingredients to create tasty treats, all with minimal effort.

1.

BEFORE YOU GET STARTED

Hand Mixer Vs. Stand Mixer – Which is Better for Baking?

Are you all mixed up and wondering: hand mixer versus stand mixer – does it really matter which one you use when baking? There are noticeable differences in the way this appliances function. Here we explain the differences, advantages and drawbacks to owning and using both.

Hand Mixer – Small and light, a hand mixer is easy to store and portable so you can mix at the stove top, sink or counter using any of your own bowls or pots. It's usually easier to operate than fancier stand mixers and it's less expensive and easier to clean. On the downside, you can't walk away from it while it's mixing and sometimes it takes longer to mix.

Stand Mixer – You'll have more speed and power with a stand mixer which you often need for big batches of dough or baking several desserts at once. It's hands-free, allowing you to multi-task while it does its job. A stand mixer also has many attachments like a paddle for creaming and a whisk for whipping egg whites. Yet, you are paying for the benefits of a stand mixer, both in price and the room needed in your kitchen to store it. Plus – they can be really heavy.

The Whisk Attachment

Whipping and Beating

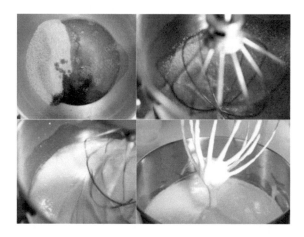

The first job that a stand mixer excels at is whipping the daylights out of stuff, whether it's cream or egg whites. It's great for aerating fluid mixtures—the stand mixer's large and open balloon whisk, when combined with the motor's power, produces more voluminous whipped cream and meringues than the narrow tines of a traditional whisk or the beaters of a hand mixer.

While it's a relatively simple matter to whip cream or egg whites by hand, there are times when the stand mixer's formidable power is particularly useful. French buttercream, for instance, requires whipping egg yolks, which is mechanically intensive.

We shouldn't undersell the ease with which a stand mixer whips things, either. Whipped egg whites aren't just for meringues; they also play a crucial role in any soufflé, whether sweet or savory, since the air trapped in the whites is what gives soufflés their airy lift.

How Do Stand Mixers Work?

The Paddle Attachment

As opposed to the whisk, which is meant for cutting through mixtures, the wide, flat blades of a paddle attachment are designed to smear and fold, which makes it invaluable for processes like creaming.

Creaming

The goal of creaming is to repeatedly fold a combination of butter and sugar until you've created an expansive network of fat, air, and sugar crystals. The more air that's trapped within the network, the greater your volume of dough will be (which means more cookies!), and the better your cakes, like this classic vanilla cake, will rise.

It's technically possible to cream butter and sugar manually, but it's incredibly labor- and time-intensive. And while any electrical mixing appliance will take care of the job in a fraction of the time, a powerful stand mixer has another advantage: temperature control. Creaming only works if the butter can stretch and expand, which means keeping it at or below 68°F, which is why bakers prefer to start with cool butter and cream as quickly as possible. You can attempt this with a hand mixer, but since they generally only work on softer, warmer butter, the results won't be nearly as foolproof.

Mixing

The paddle is a great way to uniformly mix cookie doughs and cake batters. A badly mixed cookie dough will result in a few misshapen and malformed cookies, while a poorly mixed cake will rise (and look) funny. Meanwhile, recipes like cream cheese frostings benefit from being mixed by the paddle's wide, flat blades—the thin tines of a whisk will leave you with a mound of cottage cheese–like curds instead of a smooth, airy, and light frosting that you can easily manipulate into beautiful swoops and whorls.

Mixing Meat

Because the paddle does not cut so much as it smears and folds, it's also a great way to mix and emulsify meat for dishes like sausage. A food processor, by way of comparison, cuts and chops while it mixes, and breaking the meat's protein strands will directly impact the texture of your final product (for more info, check out Kenji's article on the science of sausage and salt). If you want to start making sausages (like Italian sausage, chorizo, or merguez) at home, a stand mixer is key: It helps to knead the meat—and, crucially, does so quickly enough to avoid melting its fat content—for sausages that are juicy and springy, rather than dry and crumbly.

The Dough Hook

Finally, there's the dough hook. Making bread is certainly doable without a stand mixer and dough hook attachment, but high-fat doughs like brioche are extremely difficult to make without them. And while some doughs are actually better when made in a food processor, like Sicilian pizza dough, others really do benefit from being spun around by the dough hook, like Neapolitan-style pizza dough. Then there are breads like the simple crusty white bread; though its possible to incorporate ingredients and knead the dough by hand, it's far simpler use the dough hook for both steps (and far less messy, for what it's worth).

The benefits of using the dough hook aren't just about convenience. The relatively slower speed at which it kneads (compared to, say, a food processor) means there's little risk of over-kneading or overheating, which means you don't have to watch it like a hawk; you can clean up your kitchen or prep other things while your dough is in the stand mixer. Using the dough hook also allows you to adjust your dough when necessary, adding water or flour if it looks a little too dry or wet, respectively, and it's great for adding mix-ins, like nuts or dried fruit.

Maintenance

For the best results, always make sure that the bottom of the attachment is touching the mixing bowl. This may require some adjustment, depending on your machine. Also periodically check your mixer for loose screws, tightening as necessary.

Vibrations in the machine can loosen them over time. Inspect the bottom of the mixing bowls for undue wear and tear, that would prevent them from locking into the base. They may need replacement when they fit loosely or rattle when attached to the base.

Cleaning

Most stand mixers come equipped with a stainless steel mixing bowl, but some brands are revisiting glass, copper, or porcelain in their latest versions. All are fine choices, but some may require a little more care than stainless steel. Most mixer parts, including the bowl, can be washed safely in a dishwasher, or by hand.

After every use, go over the stand mixer itself with a damp cloth to clean any spatter on the undersides of the machine. Make sure your mixer, mixing bowl, and attachments are all free of dust and dirt before starting a new project.

2.

QUICK AND EASY RECIPES

Homemade Whipped Cream

Prep Time: 10 mins Total Time: 10 mins

Servings: 2 cups

1 cup (240g) heavy cream or heavy whipping cream

1 Tablespoon (8g or 13g) sugar

½ to 1 teaspoon vanilla extract

Preparation

Pour the heavy whipping cream, sugar, and vanilla extract into the bowl of a stand mixer fitted with the whisk attachment.

Turn the mixer to medium speed (KitchenAid stand mixer speed 4 or 5, handheld mixer speed 2 or 3). The mixture will start to get frothy and bubbly. After about 2 to 3 minutes, the mixture will start to thicken.

Once mixture is visibly thick (you will be able to see the trail of the whisk), increase the speed to medium-high (KitchenAid speed 7 or 8, handheld mixer speed 4 or 5) and beat for an additional 30 seconds to 1 minute. At this point, your whipped cream should start to look "billowy" and the trails from your whisk will be quite distinct.

Pull the whisk out of the bowl and check that the whipped cream in the bowl has formed what are called "stiff peaks." This is just a fancy term for "the whipped cream stays standing up when you pull something out of it."

Double check that your whipped cream is done by removing the whisk and flipping it upside down. If the peak stays tall without drooping off, it's done. If it's still a bit droopy, put the whisk attachment back on the mixer and beat another 10-15 seconds on medium-high (KitchenAid speed 7 or 8, handheld mixer speed 4 or 5) until stiff peaks form, checking after each 10-15 second increment.

Use immediately on your favorite dessert. Store whipped cream covered tightly in the refrigerator up to 2 days. See notes2 for freezing instructions.

Buttercream Frosting

Prep Time: 15 mins Total Time: 15 mins

Servings: 2

Plain Buttercream

2 Sticks Salted Butter, room temperature

3 Cups Powdered Sugar

For Maple Buttercream

6 Tb Pure Maple Syrup

Additional 1/2 Cup Powdered Sugar

Preparation

In a stand mixer fitted with the whisk attachment {the paddle attachment works too}, whip the butter for 30 seconds.

Add the powdered sugar 1 cup at a time. Scrape the sides in between each addition and start mixing slow then increase to medium/high. Mix for 30 seconds between each sugar addition.

{3 cups for plain frosting or 3.5 cups for maple buttercream}

Stop and scrape down sides. Add the maple syrup now if doing so.

{1-2 tsp of vanilla paste or extract can be added for vanilla buttercream frosting}

Mix on medium/high speed for 3-4 minutes. Frosting will be light and creamy.

Chill in the refrigerator for 5 minutes before frosting your cake.

Store leftover frosting in an airtight container in the refrigerator.

French Meringue

2 egg whites 65-70gr, at room temperature

¼ teaspoon cream of tartar optional

¼ teaspoon coarse kosher salt

75 gr 1/3 cup + 2 tablespoons fine granulated sugar

Preparation

In a clean mixing bowl with a whisk attachment, beat the egg whites on medium low speed until foamy. (I set it to speed 2 or 4 on my KitchenAid stand mixer.)

When egg whites are foamy, add cream of tartar and salt and continue to whisk.

Then slowly add sugar one tablespoon at a time, while mixer is still running. Allow the sugar to dissolve after each addition.

Continue beating the egg whites on the same medium low speed until desired stage is reached. About 5 minutes for soft peak stage, and 10-12 minutes for stiff peaks.

Pastry Cream

Prep: 10 minutes Infuse: 20 minutes Cook: 5 minutes

Makes 500 ml

500 ml milk

1 vanilla pod

6 egg yolks

125 g sugar

40 g flour or cornflour

Preparation

Bring the milk to the boil with the split vanilla pod. Remove from the heat and leave to infuse for 20 minutes. Beat the egg yolks and sugar in the mixer bowl with the wire whisk on speed 6 for 2 minutes until very pale and thick. Sieve over the flour or cornflour and beat until well-blended.

Bring the milk back to the boil, remove the vanilla pod and slowly pour onto the creamed mixture. Mix with the wire whisk on speed 1 until amalgamated. Pour the cream back into the saucepan and cook on a low heat, stirring with a wooden spoon until the cream comes to the boil and starts to thicken. Gently simmer for 1 minute to cook out the flour, stirring all the time. Remove from the heat, transfer to a bowl and cover the surface with clingfilm to prevent a skin from forming on the surface as it cools.

Chocolate Ganache

Prep: 2 minutes Cook: 5 minutes

Makes 250 ml

150 g dark chocolate (70%)

100 ml double cream

Preparation

Grate the chocolate with the coarse shredding drum on the rotor vegetable slicer/shredder on speed 4. Place in a heatproof bowl. Bring the cream to the boil on a low heat. Pour onto the chocolate and leave for 2 minutes, then stir gently until the chocolate has melted. Leave to cool.

Variations

Milk chocolate and nutmeg ganache

Replace the dark chocolate with 165 g milk chocolate and add ¼ to ½ teaspoon freshly grated nutmeg.

White chocolate and rose liqueur ganache

Replace the dark chocolate with 175 g white chocolate, and add 1 to 2 tablespoons of rose liqueur when the ganache is still warm but not hot.

Tomato Sauce

Prep: 5 minutes Cook: 50 minutes

Serves 4

2 onions	1 tsp dried oregano
1 celery stalk	¼ tsp chilli flakes (optional)
1 carrot	1 bay leaf
2 garlic cloves	1 sprig of rosemary
100 ml olive oil	2 tbsp tomato purée
1 kg ripe plum tomatoes,	a pinch of sugar (optional)
or 800 g tinned plum tomatoes	salt and freshly ground black pepper

Preparation

Chop the vegetables and garlic with the medium shredding drum on the rotor vegetable slicer/ shredder on speed 4. Heat the olive oil in a large saucepan and sauté the vegetables and garlic for 5 minutes until softened.

Purée the tomatoes into the mixer bowl with the coarse grinding plate on the food grinder on speed 4. Add to the pan with the herbs and tomato purée. Add a pinch of sugar, if necessary. Season and simmer for 45 minutes until the sauce has thickened and intensified in flavour.

Shortcrust Pastry

Prep: 10 minutes Chill: 30 minutes

Makes about 300 g

(enough for 1 large tart or 6 small tartlets)

200 g flour

¼ tsp salt

2 tbsp icing sugar (for Sweet shortcrust pastry)

100 g cold butter

1 beaten egg

1 tsp lemon juice

1-2 tbsp iced water

Preparation

Place the flour, salt and icing sugar (if using) in the mixer bowl. Dice the butter and add to the bowl. Mix with the flat beater on speed 2 until the mixture resembles breadcrumbs.

Add the egg, lemon juice and iced water. Continue to knead until a smooth dough is formed. Turn out onto a lightly floured surface and knead briefly. Shape into a ball, wrap in clingfilm and chill for at least 30 minutes.

Shortbread Pastry

Makes about 350 g

(enough for 1 large tart or 6 small tartlets)

Prep: 10 minutes Chill: 2 hours

100 g softened butter

75 g icing sugar

1 egg yolk

½ tsp vanilla extract

150 g flour

Preparation

Beat the butter and icing sugar in the mixer bowl with the flat beater on speed 2 until creamy and well-blended. Add the egg yolk and vanilla and mix for 10 seconds. Sieve the flour and mix in on speed 1. Turn out onto a floured surface and shape into a ball. Wrap the pastry in clingfilm and chill for at least 2 hours.

Mayonnaise

Prep: 10 minutes

Makes 250 ml

1 large egg

1 egg yolk

1 tsp lemon juice, plus extra if needed

1 tsp Dijon mustard

100 ml olive oil

100 ml groundnut oil

salt and freshly ground black pepper

Preparation

Warm the mixer bowl and wire whisk under hot running water, then dry thoroughly. Make sure all the ingredients are at room temperature, otherwise the mayonnaise will split. Place the egg, egg yolk, lemon juice and mustard in the mixer bowl. Whisk with the wire whisk on speed 8 until well-combined and frothy.

Mix the oils in a measuring jug, then add the oil to the bowl while the motor is running: drop by drop at first, then in a thin stream as the mayonnaise begins to thicken. When all the oil has been absorbed, season the mayonnaise and sharpen with extra lemon juice if necessary. This mayonnaise will not thicken as much as a mayonnaise prepared with only egg yolks.

Pesto

Prep: 10 minutes

Makes 200 ml

30 g Parmesan cheese

30 g Pecorino Romano

60 g fresh basil

40 g toasted pine nuts

2 garlic cloves

120 ml extra virgin olive oil

salt and freshly ground black pepper

Preparation

Grate the cheeses with the fine shredding drum on the rotor vegetable slicer/shredder on speed 4.

Place the basil, pine nuts and garlic in the blender, and blend to a purée on stir speed; make sure that the pesto retains some texture. With the motor running, gradually add the olive oil until all the oil has been absorbed. Scrape the mixture into a bowl and fold in the cheese. Season to taste but be careful with the salt, as the cheese is quite salty. Use immediately, or cover with a thin layer of olive oil and store in the refrigerator.

3. BREAD

Gluten-Free Coconut Bread

8 servings

Nonstick vegetable oil spray

1 cup unsweetened shredded coconut

1½ cups white rice flour

¾ cup sorghum flour

¾ cup tapioca starch

1½ teaspoons baking powder

1½ teaspoons baking soda

¾ teaspoon kosher salt

½ teaspoon xanthan gum

1½ cups sugar

1½ cups unsweetened coconut milk

¾ cup vegetable oil

1 teaspoon coconut extract (optional)

4 large eggs

¼ cup unsweetened coconut flakes

Ingredient Info:

Xanthan gum can be found at natural foods stores, some supermarkets, and online.

Preparation

Place a rack in middle of oven; preheat to 350°. Line a 9x5" loaf pan with parchment, leaving overhang on long sides; coat with nonstick spray (to use an 8½x4½" pan, hold back 1 cup batter). Toast shredded coconut on a rimmed baking sheet, tossing occasionally, until lightly browned, 5–7 minutes. Let cool.

Whisk rice flour, sorghum flour, tapioca starch, baking powder, baking soda, salt, and xanthan gum in a medium bowl. Using an electric mixer on medium speed, beat sugar, coconut milk, oil, and coconut extract, if using, in a large bowl until sugar is dissolved and mixture is smooth, about 4 minutes. Add eggs one at a time, beating well after each addition. Beat mixture until very smooth, about 2 minutes. Reduce speed to low; beat in dry ingredients. Increase speed to medium; beat batter 5 minutes. Beat in toasted coconut. Scrape batter into prepared pan; top with coconut flakes.

Bake bread until top springs back when gently pressed and a tester inserted all the way to the bottom comes out with just a few moist crumbs attached, 80–95 minutes. Transfer pan to a wire rack and let bread cool in pan 10 minutes. Turn out bread onto rack and let cool completely.

Do Ahead: Bread can be baked 4 days ahead. Store tightly wrapped at room temperature.

Milk Bread

Makes 6 rolls, one 9x5" loaf

5⅓ cups bread flour, divided, plus more for surface

1 cup heavy cream

⅓ cup mild honey (such as wildflower or alfalfa)

3 tablespoons nonfat dry milk powder

2 tablespoons active dry yeast (from about 3 envelopes)

2 tablespoons kosher salt

3 large eggs

4 tablespoons (½ stick) unsalted butter, cut into pieces, room temperature

Nonstick vegetable oil spray

Flaky sea salt (optional)

Preparation

Cook ⅓ cup flour and 1 cup water in a small saucepan over medium heat, whisking constantly, until a thick paste forms (almost like a roux but looser), about 5 minutes. Add cream and honey and cook, whisking to blend, until honey dissolves.

Transfer mixture to the bowl of a stand mixer fitted with a dough hook and add milk powder, yeast, kosher salt, 2 eggs, and 5 cups flour. Knead on medium speed until dough is smooth, about 5 minutes. Add butter, a piece at a time, fully incorporating into dough before adding the next piece, until dough is smooth, shiny, and elastic, about 4 minutes.

Coat a large bowl with nonstick spray and transfer dough to bowl, turning to coat. Cover with plastic wrap and let rise in a warm, draft-free place until doubled in size, about 1 hour.

If making rolls, lightly coat a 6-cup jumbo muffin pan with nonstick spray. Turn out dough onto a floured surface and divide into 6 pieces. Divide each piece into 4 smaller pieces (you should have 24 total). They don't need to be exact; just eyeball it. Place 4 pieces of dough side-by-side in each muffin cup.

If making a loaf, lightly coat a 9x5" loaf pan with nonstick spray. Turn out dough onto a floured surface and divide into 6 pieces. Nestle pieces side-by-side to create 2 rows down length of pan.

If making split-top buns, lightly coat two 13x9" baking dishes with nonstick spray. Divide dough into 12 pieces and shape each into a 4"-long log. Place 6 logs in a row down length of each dish.

Let shaped dough rise in a warm, draft-free place until doubled in size (dough should be just puffing over top of pan), about 1 hour.

Preheat oven to 375°. Beat remaining egg with 1 tsp. water in a small bowl to blend. Brush top of dough with egg wash and sprinkle with sea salt, if desired. Bake, rotating pan halfway through, until bread is deep golden brown, starting to pull away from the sides of the pan, and is baked through, 25–35 minutes for rolls, 50–60 minutes for loaf, or 30–40 minutes for buns. If making buns, slice each bun down the middle deep enough to create a split-top. Let milk bread cool slightly in pan on a wire rack before turning out; let cool completely.

Do Ahead: Bread can be baked 5 days ahead; store tightly wrapped at room temperature.

Classic Focaccia Bread

Makes one 18x13" pan

6¼ cups bread flour (30 oz. or 850g)

2¼ tsp. active dry yeast (from one ¼-oz. packet)

Pinch of sugar

2 Tbsp. Diamond Crystal or 1 Tbsp. Morton kosher salt

5 Tbsp. extra-virgin olive oil, divided, plus more for greasing and drizzling

Flaky sea salt

Preparation

Combine flour and 2½ cups room-temperature water in the bowl of a stand mixer fitted with the dough hook. Mix on low speed, scraping down sides and hook as needed to incorporate any dry flour, until a shaggy dough forms. Remove dough hook and cover with cloth bowl cover. Let sit while you prepare the yeast (you can leave the dough in this state up to 2 hours).

Stir yeast, sugar, and ½ cup warm water with a fork in a small bowl to dissolve. Let sit until yeast is foamy, about 5 minutes.

Pour yeast mixture into stand mixer bowl and mix on low speed until dough absorbs all additional water, about 1 minute (pulse mixer on and off a couple of times at very beginning to prevent liquid from splashing over the sides). Add kosher salt and continue to mix, increasing speed to medium, until dough is extremely elastic and very sticky (it will look more like a thick batter and will stick to sides of bowl), about 5 minutes.

Pour 3 Tbsp. oil into a large (preferably glass) bowl and swirl to coat sides. Scrape in dough with a large spatula or flexible bench scraper. Cover and place in a warm spot until dough is doubled in volume, 2–3 hours. If using a glass bowl, it's helpful to mark the position of the dough at the beginning so you can accurately assess the rise (a dry-erase marker or piece of tape works).

Drizzle 2 Tbsp. oil over an 18x13" sheet pan and use fingertips to rub all over bottom and sides. Using large spatula or flexible bench scraper, fold dough inside bowl a couple of times to deflate, then scrape onto prepared baking sheet. Using oiled hands, lift up dough and fold over onto itself in half, then rotate baking sheet 90° and fold in half again. Cover dough with a piece of well-oiled plastic and let rest 10 minutes to let gluten relax.

Uncover and go back in with oiled hands, gently stretching dough (to avoid tearing) across length and width of baking sheet in an even layer, working all the way to edges and into corners. If dough starts to spring back, let sit 5–10 minutes and start again. Cover again with same piece of oiled plastic and chill at least 8 hours and up to 24.

Let sheet pan sit in a warm spot until dough is puffed and bubbly and nearly doubled in height, 45–65 minutes (if you're using a standard half sheet pan, it will have risen to the very top of the sides). Meanwhile, place a rack in center of oven; preheat to 450°.

Remove plastic and drizzle dough generously with more oil. Oil hands again and press fingertips firmly into dough, pushing down all the way to the bottom of pan to dimple all over. Sprinkle generously with sea salt.

Bake focaccia until surface is deep golden brown all over, 25–35 minutes. Let cool in pan 10 minutes. Slide a thin metal spatula underneath focaccia to loosen from sheet pan (it may stick in a couple of places, so use some elbow grease to get underneath) and transfer to a wire rack. Let cool completely before cutting as desired.

Do Ahead: Focaccia can be baked 1 day ahead. Tightly wrap in plastic and store at room temperature.

Anadama Bread

Makes 1 loaf

2 tablespoons unsalted butter, room temperature, plus more

1 ¼-ounce envelope active dry yeast (about 2¼ tsp.)

1 cup stone-ground medium cornmeal

¼ cup mild-flavored (light) molasses

2 tablespoons hemp seeds or white sesame seeds

1 tablespoon nigella seeds or black sesame seeds

2 teaspoons golden flaxseed

2 teaspoons brown flaxseed

2 teaspoons poppy seeds

1¼ teaspoon kosher salt

2 cups all-purpose flour, plus more for surface

1large egg, beaten to blend

Salted butter (for serving)

Preparation

Preheat oven to 375°. Lightly butter an 8x4" loaf pan and line with parchment paper, leaving generous overhang. Place yeast in a medium bowl (or the bowl of a stand mixer) and add 1 cup warm water; stir to dissolve yeast. Add cornmeal, molasses, hemp seeds, nigella seeds, golden and brown flaxseed, poppy seeds, salt, 2 cups flour, and 2 Tbsp. unsalted butter. Using a wooden spoon (or dough hook if using stand mixer), mix until no dry spots remain.

Turn out dough onto a lightly floured surface and knead until dough is smooth and elastic, 10–15 minutes (alternatively, mix in stand mixer on medium speed 8–10 minutes). Lightly butter a medium bowl. Transfer dough to bowl and turn to coat. Cover with plastic wrap and let rise in a warm, draft-free spot until almost doubled in size, about 1 hour.

Punch down dough to deflate; cover. Let rise again until about doubled in size, about 1 hour.

Turn out dough onto a lightly floured surface and pat into an 8x4" rectangle. Starting at the short side farthest from you, roll up dough, pinching the seam as you go, to create a tight roll. Pinch seam to close; tuck ends under and pinch to seal. Place seam side down in prepared pan and cover with plastic. Let dough rises until it crests the top of the pan and springs back slightly when pressed, about 1 hour.

Brush top of dough with egg. Bake, rotating halfway through, until bread is baked through and top is a deep golden brown, 45–50 minutes. Let cool slightly in pan on a wire rack before turning out. Let cool before slicing (if you can wait that long). Serve with salted butter.

Do Ahead: Bread can be made 5 days ahead. Store tightly wrapped at room temperature.

Best Banana Bread

Makes one 8½x4½" loaf

Nonstick vegetable oil spray

1½ cups all-purpose flour

1¼ teaspoons baking soda

¾ teaspoon kosher salt

1 cup (packed) dark brown sugar

⅓ cup mascarpone, plain whole-milk Greek yogurt, or sour cream

¼ cup (½ stick) unsalted butter, room temperature

28

2 large eggs

4 large very ripe bananas, mashed (about 1½ cups)

½ cup chopped bittersweet or semisweet chocolate (optional)

½ cup chopped walnuts (optional)

Preparation

Preheat oven to 350°. Lightly coat 8½x4½" loaf pan with nonstick spray and line with parchment paper, leaving a generous overhang on long sides. Whisk flour, baking soda, and salt in a medium bowl.

Using an electric mixer on medium-high speed, beat brown sugar, mascarpone, and butter in a large bowl until light and fluffy, about 4 minutes. Add eggs one at a time, beating to blend after each addition and scraping down sides and bottom of bowl as needed.

Reduce speed to low, add dry ingredients, and mix until just combined. Add mashed bananas and mix just until combined. Fold in chocolate and/or walnuts, if using. Scrape batter into prepared loaf pan; smooth top.

Bake bread until a tester inserted into the center comes out clean, 60–65 minutes. Transfer pan to a wire rack and let the bread cool in pan 1 hour. Turn out bread and let cool completely (if you can resist) before slicing.

Pão de Queijo (Brazilian Cheese Bread)

Pão de queijo, which means "cheese bread" in Portuguese, is a delightful snack from Brazil made with tapioca flour (meaning it's gluten-free) and cheese. Our recipe calls for both Parmesan, which adds a sharp and salty flavor, and farmer's cheese, which is creamy and milky. You definitely want both!

Makes about 18

½ cup whole milk

¼ cup (½ stick) unsalted butter

1½ teaspoons kosher salt

2 cups tapioca flour

2 large eggs

5 ounces fresh farmer's cheese, crumbled (about 1 cup)

2 ounces crumbled Parmesan (about ½ cup)

Preparation

Arrange a rack in center of oven; preheat to 425°. Heat milk, butter, salt, and ¼ cup water in a large saucepan over medium-high, stirring occasionally, until butter is melted and mixture begins to boil, about 4 minutes. Remove from heat and add flour; vigorously stir with a wooden spoon until dough is dry and shaggy, about 10 seconds. Transfer to the bowl of a stand mixer fitted with the paddle attachment or a large bowl. Let cool for 5 minutes.

Beat mixture on low-speed just until the dough starts to come together, about 30 seconds (alternatively, vigorously stir with a wooden spoon). Add eggs, one at a time, and continue to beat on low speed until incorporated (dough will look broken at first, then come together). Continue to beat on low speed until dough is smooth, sticky, and somewhat stretchy; do not overbeat or dough will lose its stretch. Add farmer cheese and Parmesan and beat on low speed until evenly distributed.

30

Using a 1⅓-oz. ice cream scoop, portion dough and transfer to a parchment-lined rimmed baking sheet, spacing about 2" apart (alternatively, form dough into ping pong ball-sized pieces with your hands).

Bake 5 minutes, then reduce oven temperature to 350° and continue to bake until pão are very light brown, with some darker brown speckles all over (that's the cheese), and sound hollow when tapped on the bottom, 20–25 minutes. Let cool 10 minutes before serving.

Homemade Bagels

Prep Time: 2 hours, 10 minutes Cook Time: 25 minutes Total Time: 3 hours

Yield: 8 bagels

1 and 1/2 cups (360ml) warm water (between 100-110°F, 38-43°C)

2 and 3/4 teaspoons instant or active dry yeast

4 cups (520g) bread flour (spoon & leveled), plus more for work surface and hands

1 Tablespoon granulated sugar or packed light or dark brown sugar (or barley malt syrup)

2 teaspoons salt

coating the bowl: nonstick spray or 2 teaspoons olive oil

egg wash: 1 egg white beaten with 1 Tablespoon water

For Boiling:

2 quarts water

1/4 cup (60g) honey

Preparation

Prepare the dough: Whisk the warm water and yeast together in the bowl of your stand mixer fitted with a dough hook attachment. Cover and allow to sit for 5 minutes.

Add the flour, brown sugar, and salt. Beat on low speed for 2 minutes. The dough is very stiff and will look somewhat dry.

Turn the dough out onto a lightly floured surface. With lightly floured hands, knead the dough for 6-7 minutes. After kneading, the dough should still feel a little soft. Poke it with your finger—if it slowly bounces back, your dough is ready to rise. If not, keep kneading. The dough is too heavy for the mixer to knead it.

Lightly grease a large bowl with oil or nonstick spray. Place the dough in the bowl, turning it to coat all sides in the oil. Cover the bowl with aluminum foil, plastic wrap, or a clean kitchen towel. Allow the dough to rise at room temperature for 60-90 minutes or until double in size.

Line two large baking sheets with parchment paper or silicone baking mats.

Shape the bagels: When the dough is ready, punch it down to release any air bubbles. Divide the dough into 8 equal pieces. (Just eyeball it– doesn't need to be perfect!) Shape each piece into a ball. Press your index finger through the center of each ball to make a hole about 1.5 – 2 inches in diameter. Watch video below for a visual. Loosely cover the shaped bagels with kitchen towel and rest for a few minutes as you prepare the water bath.

Preheat oven to 425°F (218°C).

Water bath: Fill a large, wide pot with 2 quarts of water. Whisk in the honey. Bring water to a boil, then reduce heat to medium-high. Drop bagels in, 2-4 at a time, making sure they have enough room to float around. Cook the bagels for 1 minute on each side.

Using a pastry brush, brush the egg wash on top and around the sides of each bagel. Place 4 bagels onto each lined baking sheet.

Bake for 20-25 minutes, rotating the pan halfway through. You want the bagels to be a dark golden brown. Remove from the oven and allow bagels to cool on the baking sheets for 20 minutes, then transfer to a wire rack to cool completely.

Slice, toast, top, whatever you want! Cover leftover bagels tightly and store at room temperature for a few days or in the refrigerator for up to 1 week.

Monkey Bread

Servings: 8

Dough:

¼ cup (57 g) butter divided, 2 tablespoons softened and 2 tablespoons melted

1 cup milk, warm (about 110 degrees)

⅓ cup water, warm (about 110 degrees)

¼ cup (53 g) granulated sugar

2 ¼ teaspoons instant yeast

3 ¼ cups (462 g) all-purpose flour, plus extra for work surface

2 teaspoons salt

Brown Sugar Coating:

1 cup (212 g) packed light brown sugar

2 teaspoons ground cinnamon

½ cup (113 g) butter, melted

Glaze:

1 cup (114 g) confectioners' sugar

2 tablespoons milk

Preparation

Butter a Bundt pan with the 2 tablespoons softened butter. Use a pastry brush or a paper towel or anything that will really help get inside all of those nooks and crannies. Set aside.

In a large measuring cup, mix together the milk, water, melted butter, sugar, and yeast. Mix the flour and salt together in a standing mixer fitted with dough hook. Turn the machine to low and slowly add the milk mixture. After the dough comes together, increase the speed to medium and mix until the dough is shiny and smooth, 6 to 7 minutes. If you think the dough is too wet (i.e. having a hard time forming a cohesive mass), add 2 tablespoons flour at a time and mix until the dough comes together (it should still be on the sticky side, just not overly wet).

Coat a large bowl with nonstick cooking spray. Place the dough in the bowl and turn to coat lightly with the cooking spray. Cover the bowl with plastic wrap and let the dough rise until doubled, 1-2 hours (alternately, you can preheat the oven to 200 degrees, turning it off once it reaches 200 degrees and place the covered bowl in the oven to speed up the rising time).

For the sugar coating, while the dough is rising, mix the brown sugar and cinnamon together in a bowl. Place the melted butter in a second bowl or shallow pie plate. Set aside.

To form the bread, gently remove the dough from the bowl and press it into a rough 8-inch square. Using a bench scraper or knife, cut the dough into 64 pieces.

Roll each dough piece into a ball (it doesn't have to be perfect, just get it into a rough ball-shape). Working one at a time, dip the balls in melted butter, allowing excess butter to drip back into the bowl or pie plate. Roll the dipped dough ball in the brown sugar mixture, then layer the balls in the Bundt pan, staggering the seams where the dough balls meet as you build layers.

Cover the Bundt pan tightly with plastic wrap and let the monkey bread rise until puffy and they have risen 1-2 inches from the top of the pan, 1-2 hours (again, you can use the warm oven approach to speed this up).

Heat the oven to 350 degrees F (remove the pan from the oven if you placed it there to rise). Unwrap the pan and bake until the top is deep brown and caramel begins to bubble around edges, 30 to 35 minutes. Cool the monkey bread in the pan for 5 minutes (any longer and the bread will be too sticky and hard to remove!), then turn out on a platter or large plate and allow to cool slightly, about 10 minutes.

For the glaze, while the bread cools, whisk the confectioners' sugar and milk together in a small bowl until the mixture is smooth. Using a whisk, drizzle the glaze over the warm monkey bread, letting it run over the top and sides of the bread. Serve warm.

Rosemary Focaccia Bread

This Rosemary Focaccia Bread recipe is ultra-comforting and delicious, and kicked up a notch with the addition of lots of fresh rosemary and flaked sea salt. See optional instructions below for how to mix the dough by hand if you do not have a stand mixer.

Prep Time: 75 Minutes Cook Time: 20 Minutes Total Time: 95 Minutes

Servings: 8 -12

1 1/3 cup warm water (about 110°F)

2 teaspoons sugar or honey

1 (0.25 ounce) package active-dry yeast

3 1/2 cups all purpose flour

1/4 cup extra virgin olive oil, plus more for drizzling

2 teaspoons flaky sea salt, plus extra for sprinkling

2 sprigs fresh rosemary

Preparation

Proof the yeast. Add warm water (about 110°F, which you can measure with a thermometer if you want to be sure it's the right temp) and sugar to the bowl of a stand mixer with the dough attachment, and stir to combine. Sprinkle the yeast on top of the water. Give the yeast a quick stir to mix it in with the water. Then let it sit for 5-10 minute until the yeast is foamy.

Knead the dough. (See alterate instructions below to knead by hand.) Set the mixer to low speed, and add gradually flour, olive oil and salt. Increase speed to medium-low, and continue mixing the dough for 5 minutes. (If the dough is too sticky and isn't pulling away from the sides of the bowl, add in an extra 1/4 cup flour while it is mixing.)

First dough rise. Remove dough from the mixing bowl, and use your hands to shape it into a ball. Grease the mixing bowl (or a separate bowl) with olive oil or cooking spray, then place the dough ball back in the bowl and cover it with a damp towel.

Place in a warm location (I set mine by a sunny window) and let the dough rise for 45-60 minutes, or until it has nearly doubled in size.

Second dough rise. Turn the dough onto a floured surface, and roll it out into a large circle or rectangle until that the dough is about 1/2-inch thick*. Cover the dough again with the damp towel, and let the dough continue to rise for another 20 minutes.

Prepare the dough. Preheat oven to 400°F. Transfer the dough to a large parchment-covered baking sheet (or press it into a 9 x 13-inch baking dish). Use your fingers to poke deep dents (seriously, poke all the way down to the baking sheet!) all over the surface of the dough. Drizzle a tablespoon or two of olive oil evenly all over the top of the dough, and sprinkle evenly with the fresh rosemary needles and sea salt.

Bake. Bake for 20 minutes, or until the dough is slightly golden and cooked through.

Serve. Remove from the oven, and drizzle with a little more olive oil if desired. Slice, and serve warm.

Challah

Prep Time: 3 hours Cook Time: 30 mins Total Time: 3 hours 30 minutes

Yield: 2 loaves 1x

2 ¼ tsp dry yeast	**¼ cup olive or vegetable oil**
1 ½ cups water	**1 tsp salt**
1 tsp sugar	**1 egg yolk**
2 eggs	**6 cups flour**
½ cup sugar	

Preparation

Add the yeast to a small bowl with ¼ cup warm (105-115 F) water, with 1 teaspoon sugar dissolved into it. Let proof until foamy (5 minutes).

In the bowl of a stand mixer, combine the eggs, ½ cup sugar, oil, and 1 ⅓ cups water. Mix until homogenous, then add the proofed yeast mixture. Mix again.

In a separate bowl, combine the flour and salt, then add to the wet mixture and mix to combine before using a dough hook (or kneading by hands) until the mixture is completely smooth. It should not be sticky. In my KitchenAid mixer I let the dough hook work for about 7 minutes.

Place the dough in a lightly oiled bowl and cover with plastic wrap, then a kitchen towel. Let rise in a warm place (I use the oven with the light on) until doubled in size, 1.5-2 hours.

When the dough has risen, punch it down and turn out onto a lightly floured surface. Divide into two pieces, and let them rest for 10 minutes.

Divide each piece into three equal pieces (you'll have six total now), and form into long ropes about 1" thick. You'll be making two loaves, so braid three together, pinching the ends and tucking them under.

Set on a parchment-lined baking sheet, or lightly oiled baking sheet.

Let the loaves rise for 1 hour.

Preheat the oven to 350 F.

Brush the loaves with the egg yolk mixed with 1 tablespoon water, and sprinkle with poppy seeds if you want.

Bake for 30 minutes. Challah should be golden and sound hollow when tapped.

4. COOKIES

Whiskey and Rye Chocolate Chip Cookies

Mixing your two favorite pastimes: cookies and whiskey.

Makes 16 cookies

1½ cups chocolate wafers (discs, pistoles, fèves; preferably 72% cacao), divided

2 cups all-purpose flour

½ cup rye flour

½ teaspoon baking soda

1½ teaspoons kosher salt

¾ cup (1½ sticks) plus 1 tablespoon unsalted butter, room temperature

¾ cup dark brown sugar

¾ cup granulated sugar

1 large egg

1½ teaspoons vanilla extract or vanilla paste

1 teaspoon bourbon

1 vanilla bean, split lengthwise

1 teaspoon flaky sea salt

Ingredient Info

Find chocolate wafers (do not use chocolate wafer cookies) at specialty food stores, some grocery stores, and online.

Preparation

Pulse ¾ cup chocolate wafers in a food processor until pea-sized pieces form. Whisk all-purpose flour, rye flour, baking soda, and kosher salt in a medium bowl.

Using an electric mixer on medium speed, beat butter, brown sugar, and granulated sugar in a large bowl, scraping down sides of bowl as needed, until light and fluffy, 3–4 minutes. Add egg, vanilla, and bourbon and beat until fully incorporated, about 1 minute. Reduce speed to low and slowly add dry ingredients, mixing just to blend. Fold in chopped chocolate and remaining chocolate wafers.

Portion dough into 16 balls (about ¼ cup each) and transfer to a rimmed sheet sheet as you go. Wrap tightly with plastic wrap and chill at least 3 hours or up to 1 day.

Position rack in middle of oven and preheat to 350°. Scrape vanilla seeds into sea salt in a small bowl and mix to combine (save pod for another use).

Divide dough balls between 2 parchment-lined baking sheets, spacing 3" apart. Flatten each ball to about ¾" thick and sprinkle with vanilla salt. Bake cookies, rotating sheets halfway through, until golden brown around the edges, 14–18 minutes (cookies will firm up as they cool). Let cool slightly on baking sheets, then transfer to wire racks and let cool completely.

Do Ahead: Cookies can be made 1 day ahead. Store airtight at room temperature.

Rainbow Cookies

Makes 96

2 tablespoons plus 2 cups unsalted butter, cubed, at room temperature

6 large eggs, separated

1 1/3 cups sugar, divided

12 ounces almond paste (not marzipan), chopped

2 3/4 cups plus 1 tablespoon all-purpose flour

1 teaspoon red food coloring

1 teaspoon salt

3/4 cup orange marmalade, heated, strained

4 ounces bittersweet chocolate, chopped, melted

1 teaspoon green food coloring

Special Equipment: 3 13x9x2" metal baking pans

Preparation

Bake:

Preheat oven to 350° Line three 13x9x2" metal baking pans with foil, leaving overhang; grease with 2 tablespoon butter; set aside. Put egg whites in bowl of a stand mixer fitted with a whisk; beat until soft peaks form. Slowly add 1/3 cup sugar, beating until stiff peaks form. Transfer to a large bowl; cover; chill. Using the paddle attachment, beat almond paste and remaining sugar on medium-low until incorporated, 4-5 minutes. Increase speed to medium-high; gradually add remaining butter. Beat until fluffy. Beat in yolks, then flour and salt. Fold in whites in 2 additions. Divide batter evenly among 3 bowls. Mix red coloring into 1 bowl and green coloring into second bowl; leave third bowl plain. Spread 1 bowl of batter into each prepared pan; smooth tops. Bake, rotating pans halfway through, until just set, 9-11 minutes. Let cool in pans.

Layer:

With a pastry brush, spread half of marmalade over green cake. Using foil overhang, lift plain layer out of pan. Invert onto green layer; discard foil. Brush remaining marmalade over plain layer. Lift red layer out of pan; invert onto plain layer and cover cake with foil.

Weight:

Top with a 13x9x2" pan. Weigh down pan with several heavy canned goods to compress cake layers. Refrigerate at least 4 hours and up to 1 day.

Unmold:

Remove cans, top pan, and foil. Transfer cake to a waxed paper-lined baking sheet.

Glaze:

Spread half of chocolate over cake in a thin layer. Freeze for 10 minutes. Cover with waxed paper, invert the baking sheet on top, and flip cake. Uncover and glaze with remaining chocolate. Freeze 10 additional minutes.

Slice:

Trim cake to 12x8". Cut crosswise into six 2"-wide strips. Cut each strip crosswise into 96"-wide cookies. Store in an airtight container.

Alfajores With Coconut Dulce de Leche

The traditional South American honey-almond cookie gets a tropical twist thanks to a decadent yet shockingly easy coconut dulce de leche, oozing between two shortbread cookies. Top it with a blanket of brightly dyed coconut flakes and suddenly you're on a beach far, far away.

Makes about 24

1 14-oz. can sweetened condensed milk

1 13.5-oz. can unsweetened coconut milk

2 tsp. kosher salt, divided

½ cup (50 g) almond flour or meal

2¼ cups (288 g) all-purpose flour, plus more for dusting

1 cup (2 sticks) unsalted butter, room temperature

⅓ cup (76 g) granulated sugar

1 large egg yolk

1 tsp. vanilla extract

¼ cup plus 2 Tbsp. honey

1½ cups (125 g) unsweetened shredded coconut

1 Tbsp. (or more) any color plant-based food-coloring powder

1 Tbsp. (or more) second color plant-based food-coloring powder

Luster dust (optional)

Special Equipment: Assorted 2" (or smaller) cookie cutters

Preparation

Place a rack in the middle of oven; preheat to 375°. Bring condensed milk, coconut milk, and ½ tsp. salt to a boil in a small saucepan over medium-high heat. Scrape mixture into a 13x9" baking dish and bake, stirring every 15 minutes or so, until very thick and a light caramel color, 40–50 minutes. The mixture will look lumpy, broken, and very pasty—that's exactly what you want. Let cool in dish 1 hour, then transfer to a food processor and process until smooth. Set dulce de leche aside for serving.

Meanwhile, whisk almond flour and 2¼ cups all-purpose flour in a medium bowl to combine. Using an electric mixer on medium-high speed, beat butter, sugar, and 1½ tsp. salt in a large bowl, scraping down sides and bottom of bowl as needed, until pale and creamy, about 3 minutes. Add egg yolk, vanilla, and ¼ cup honey and beat until combined, about 2 minutes. Reduce speed to low, add dry ingredients, and mix, scraping down sides and bottom of bowl, until incorporated. Divide dough in half and pat each piece into a 1"-thick disk. Wrap in plastic and chill until firm, at least 2 hours.

Preheat oven to 350°. Roll out 1 disk of dough on a lightly floured sheet of parchment paper, dusting with more flour as needed to keep dough from sticking, to about ⅛" thick. Punch out shapes with lightly floured cookie cutters and transfer to 2 parchment-lined baking sheets, spacing 1" apart. Pat scraps into a 1"-thick disk, wrap with plastic, and chill 10 minutes if soft.

Bake a sheet of cookies, rotating halfway through, until edges are lightly browned, 7–9 minutes. Let cool 10 minutes on baking sheet, then transfer to a wire rack and let cool completely. Bake remaining sheet of cookies. Line baking sheets with fresh sheets of parchment paper and repeat process with remaining disk of dough.

Divide coconut evenly among 3 bowls. Add 1 Tbsp. food-coloring powder (sift if needed) to a bowl of coconut and toss until coconut is coated; add more powder if a more intense color is desired. Repeat with remaining food-coloring powder and another bowl of coconut. Leave 1 bowl of coconut white. If using, add some luster dust to all 3 bowls and toss to combine.

Turn half of the cookies over to expose flat side; spread 1 tsp. dulce de leche over (this will be the inside of the sandwiches); set aside.

Heat remaining 2 Tbsp. honey in a small bowl in the microwave just until warm (you want it to be loose), then stir in 2 tsp. warm water. Working one at a time, lightly brush honey over the top of remaining cookies (the ones that have not been filled with dulce de leche). Immediately dip tops into a bowl of coconut; press additional coconut onto cookie to cover any bald spots. Close up cookie sandwiches, coconut side up.

Do Ahead: Dulce de leche can be made 1 month ahead; place in an airtight container and freeze. Thaw in refrigerator overnight before using. Dough can be made 3 days ahead; keep chilled. Cookies can be baked (but not assembled) 2 days ahead; store airtight at room temperature.

Peanut Meringue Cookies

Makes about 12

1 cup plus 2 tablespoons skin-off unsalted, roasted peanuts

2 large egg whites, room temperature

1 cup powdered sugar

¼ teaspoon kosher salt

½ teaspoon vanilla extract

Preparation

Preheat oven to 350°. Spread out peanuts on a rimmed baking sheet. Using a mug or a rolling pin, crush into large bits; set aside.

Pour water into a medium saucepan to a depth of about 1" and bring to a simmer over medium. Combine egg whites, powdered sugar, and salt in the bowl of a stand mixer and set over saucepan (you want bowl to rest securely in the rim of the saucepan over, not touching, the water). Heat, whisking constantly, until whites are hot to the touch (you can check with an instant-read thermometer; it should register 120°), about 5 minutes.

Transfer bowl to stand mixer fitted with whisk attachment and beat on high speed until soft peaks form. Add vanilla and continue to beat meringue until very thick and glossy stiff peaks form, about 5 minutes total. Using a rubber spatula, fold in half of reserved peanuts, then add remaining peanuts and work in just enough to create streaks. Immediately spoon heaping tablespoons onto a parchment-lined baking sheet into 1½" mounds, spacing about 1" apart.

Place meringues in the oven and prop the door ajar with the handle of a wooden spoon. Bake meringues until they puff slightly, crack along the sides, and feel dry on the outside but soft to the touch, 15–20 minutes. Transfer meringues to a wire rack and let cool.

Do Ahead: Meringues can be made 2 days ahead. Store airtight at room temperature.

Chocolate Chip Cookies

Prep: 10 minutes Passive: 10 minutes Cook: 15 minutes

Serves 11

2 c flour

1/2 tsp baking soda

3/4 c white sugar

3/4 c brown sugar

3/4 c melted butter

1 egg + 1 yolk

1 T vanilla extract

1 bag semi sweet chocolate chips

Preparation

Preheat oven to 350

Sift together flour and baking soda in a mixing bowl, set aside.

Cream together butter and sugars in stand mixer.

Add eggs and vanilla, mix until light and blended.

Add in dry ingredients a little at a time until full combined.

Lastly, fold in the chocolate chips.

Refrigerate 10-15 minutes to help the dough firm up.

Scoop 1/4 cup size scoops, I use ice cream scoop for uniform size, and put onto greased or lined baking sheet. Leave 2 inches between each cookie.

Bake for 15-16 minutes on 350.

Chocolate-Hazelnut Cookies

Coarse raw sugar gives them a subtle crunch in every bite, but you can replace it with an equal amount of white sugar if needed. And trust us on the big pieces of chocolate: The matchsticks are what give these cookies their melty stripes.

Makes about 2½ dozen

¾ cup (115 g) blanched hazelnuts

3½ cups (440 g) all-purpose flour

1 tsp. kosher salt

¾ tsp. baking powder

½ tsp. baking soda

½ tsp. ground ginger

1 cup (2 sticks) unsalted butter, room temperature

½ cup (100 g) granulated sugar

½ cup (100 g) raw sugar or granulated sugar

½ cup (100 g) (packed) light brown sugar

2 large eggs, room temperature

¼ cup honey

½ tsp. vanilla extract

4 2-oz. bittersweet chocolate bars, cut lengthwise into ¼"-thick sticks

Flaky sea salt

Preparation

Place racks in upper and lower thirds of oven; preheat to 300°. Toast hazelnuts on a rimmed baking sheet on upper rack, tossing halfway through, until golden brown, 8–10 minutes. Let cool slightly, then chop very coarsely; set aside. Increase oven temperature to 350°.

Whisk flour, kosher salt, baking powder, baking soda, and ginger in a large bowl to combine. Beat butter, granulated sugar, raw sugar, and brown sugar in the bowl of a stand mixer fitted with the paddle attachment on high speed, scraping down sides of bowl occasionally, until pale and fluffy, 5–7 minutes. Reduce speed to medium-high and add eggs, one at a time, increasing speed to high after each addition to fully incorporate and stopping periodically to scrape down sides of bowl. Add honey and vanilla and beat just to combine. Reduce speed to low and add dry ingredients; beat until combined. Add chocolate and reserved nuts and beat just until incorporated.

Scoop dough into 1½-oz. portions (about 3 Tbsp.); roll into balls (if the batter feels loose or sticky, chill 30 minutes). Place on a parchment-lined baking sheet. Chill until firm, at least 2 hours.

Arrange chilled cookies on 2 fresh parchment-lined baking sheets, spacing 2" apart; you should be able to fit about 12 cookies on each. Sprinkle cookies with sea salt.

Bake, rotating top to bottom and front to back halfway through, until bottoms and edges are golden brown, 12–15 minutes. Let cool on baking sheets. Place a fresh sheet of parchment on 1 baking sheet and repeat process with remaining balls of dough.

Do Ahead: Dough can be made 1 month ahead. Transfer chilled balls to resealable freezer bags and freeze. Bake from frozen.

Salty Chocolate Chunk Cookies

24 Servings

1 1/2 cups all-purpose flour

1 teaspoon baking powder

1/2 teaspoon kosher salt

1/4 teaspoon baking soda

1/2 cup (1 stick) unsalted butter, room temperature

3/4 cup (packed) light brown sugar

1/2 cup sugar

1/4 cup powdered sugar

2 large egg yolks

1 large egg

1 teaspoon vanilla extract

8 ounces semisweet or bittersweet chocolate (do not exceed 72% cacao), coarsely chopped

Maldon or other flaky sea salt

Preparation

Place racks in upper and lower thirds of oven and preheat to 375°. Whisk flour, baking powder, kosher salt, and baking soda in a medium bowl; set aside.

Using an electric mixer on medium speed, beat butter, brown sugar, sugar, and powdered sugar until light and fluffy, 3-4 minutes. Add egg yolks, egg, and vanilla. Beat, occasionally scraping down the sides of the bowl, until mixture is pale and fluffy, 4-5 minutes. Reduce mixer speed to low; slowly add dry ingredients, mixing just to blend. Using a spatula, fold in chocolate.

Spoon rounded tablespoonfuls of cookie dough onto 2 parchment paper-lined baking sheets, spacing 1-inch apart. Sprinkle cookies with sea salt.

Bake cookies, rotating sheets halfway through, until just golden brown around the edges, 10-12 minutes (the cookies will firm up as they cool). Let cool slightly on baking sheets, then transfer to wire racks; let cool completely.

DO AHEAD: Cookies can be made 1 day ahead. Store airtight at room temperature.

Ancho Mole Cookies

Makes about 48

1 cup (140 g) nuts (such as blanched hazelnuts, blanched almonds, or walnuts)

1¼ cups (185 g; or more) raw sesame seeds, divided

⅓ cup (54 g) ancho powder (pure ground ancho chiles, not ancho chile powder, which has added salt, cumin, and other spices)

¼ cup agave syrup, preferably dark

2 cups (256 g) all-purpose flour

¼ tsp. baking powder

¼ tsp. ground cinnamon

12 tbsp. unsalted butter, room temperature

½ cup (100 g) sugar

1¾ tsp. kosher salt

3 large egg yolks

1 tbsp. vanilla extract or vanilla bean paste

¾ cup (130 g) dried fruit (such as papaya, mango, or pineapple), cut into ¾" pieces

¾ cup (110 g) bittersweet chocolate wafers (disks, pistoles, fèves; preferably 72% cacao)

1 large egg white, lightly beaten

Preparation

Place racks in upper and lower thirds of oven; preheat to 350°. Toast nuts and ¼ cup sesame seeds on a rimmed baking sheet on upper rack, tossing halfway through, until golden brown, 8–10 minutes. Let cool.

Stir together ancho powder and agave syrup in a small bowl. Whisk flour, baking powder, and cinnamon in a medium bowl to combine. Using an electric mixer on medium-high speed, beat butter, sugar, and salt in a large bowl, scraping down sides and bottom of bowl as needed, until light and creamy, about 3 minutes. Add egg yolks and vanilla and beat until incorporated, about 1 minute. Scrape in ancho mixture and beat until smooth and creamy, about 1 minute. Reduce speed to low, add dry ingredients, and beat to combine. Add dried fruit, chocolate, and toasted nuts and sesame seeds; mix with a wooden spoon until evenly distributed.

Divide dough in half. Working one at a time, roll each piece into a 10"-long log. Wrap each log tightly in plastic and roll across work surface to make as smooth and cylindrical as possible. Place on a rimmed baking sheet and freeze until surface is firm, about 20 minutes.

Slap a log down onto counter to create a flat side; roll over and slap again to flatten another side (you're aiming for a triangular shape). Repeat to create third side of the triangle. Tap against counter to smooth if needed, then tap ends to flatten. Repeat with second log. Return logs to baking sheet; freeze until firm, about 15 minutes.

Working one at a time, unwrap logs and brush sides with egg white. Working on baking sheet, sprinkle sides with remaining 1 cup sesame seeds and gently press to coat. Surface should be covered; use more sesame if needed. Freeze logs on baking sheet, uncovered, until surface is very firm but not frozen solid, about 1 hour.

Preheat oven to 350°. Slice a log crosswise into ¼"-thick triangles and divide cookies between 2 parchment-lined baking sheets, spacing 1" apart. (If dough is soft or starts to lose its shape, freeze 10 minutes before continuing.) Bake cookies, rotating baking sheets top to bottom and back to front halfway through, until edges are just set, about 10 minutes. Let cool on baking sheets. Transfer cookies to a platter or airtight container and line baking sheets with fresh sheets of parchment paper. Repeat process with remaining dough.

Do Ahead: Dough can be rolled into logs 3 days ahead; refrigerate. Transfer to freezer 30 minutes before slicing. Cookies can be baked 1 day ahead; store airtight at room temperature.

5. CAKES

Gluten-Free Carrot Cake

Almond flour is a wonderfully sweet, nutty complement for fresh carrots, walnuts, and raisins. If you can't find it, though, here's a trick: Use 2¼ cups whole almonds and pulse them in a food processor along with salt, baking powder, all three spices, and baking soda until very, very finely ground.

8–12 servings

CAKE

½ cup virgin coconut oil, melted, plus more for pans

3 cups almond flour, plus more for dusting pans

1½ tsp. kosher salt

1 tsp. baking powder

1 tsp. ground cardamom

1 tsp. ground cinnamon

1 tsp. ground ginger

½ tsp. baking soda

5 large eggs

1¼ cups (packed) dark brown sugar

1 tsp. vanilla extract

10 oz. carrots, peeled, coarsely shredded, squeezed firmly to expel excess water

¾ cup shredded unsweetened coconut

¾ cup walnuts, finely chopped

½ cup golden raisins

FROSTING AND ASSEMBLY

8 oz. cream cheese, room temperature

½ cup (1 stick) unsalted butter, room temperature

1¼ cups gluten-free powdered sugar

⅓ cup Greek yogurt

1 tsp. vanilla extract

Pinch of kosher salt

Preparation

CAKE

Preheat oven to 350°. Grease two 8" parchment-lined round cake pans with oil, then dust with almond flour, tapping out excess.

Whisk salt, baking powder, cardamom, cinnamon, ginger, baking soda, and remaining 3 cups flour in a medium bowl.

Using an electric mixer on medium-high speed, beat eggs and brown sugar in a large bowl until more than tripled in volume and mixture holds a ribbon for several seconds when drizzled over itself, 5–7 minutes. (Beating the eggs thoroughly in this stage goes a long way toward creating an aerated, light crumb, which is critical when using gluten-free ingredients.) Beat in vanilla.

Toss carrots, coconut, walnuts, raisins, and remaining ½ cup oil in another medium bowl.

Reduce mixer speed to low. Add flour mixture in 3 additions, alternating with carrot mixture in 3 additions, to egg mixture, beating well after each addition.

Divide batter between prepared pans. Bake cake until lightly browned across the top, a tester inserted into the center comes out clean, and the top springs back when gently poked, 33–36 minutes. Let cool 10 minutes. Carefully run a knife around edges of pans to release cake, then invert onto a wire rack. Let cool completely.

FROSTING AND ASSEMBLY

Using electric mixer on medium-high speed, beat cream cheese and butter in a large bowl, scraping down as needed, until very smooth, about 2 minutes. Reduce mixer speed to low and add powdered sugar. Beat until combined. Add yogurt, vanilla, and salt and increase speed to medium-high. Beat, scraping down occasionally, until light and airy, about 4 minutes. Chill 10 minutes if needed to stiffen slightly to a spreadable consistently.

Arrange one cake round domed side down on a large plate or platter. Cover top and sides with one-third of frosting. Top with remaining cake layer, domed side up. Coat top and sides with remaining frosting.

Do Ahead: Cake can be made 3 days ahead. Cover with a cake dome and chill.

Malted Milk Cheesecake

10 Servings

300g shortbread biscuits

80g unsalted butter, melted, cooled

1kg cream cheese, at room temperature

1/2 cup (110g) caster sugar

1 tbs cornflour

3 eggs

1 cup (110g) malted milk powder

MERINGUE

1 cup (220g) caster sugar

Pinch of cream of tartar

4 eggwhites

Preparation

Preheat the oven to 150°C. Grease and line the base and sides of a 20cm springform cake pan with baking paper, then place on a baking tray.

Place biscuits in a food processor and whiz to fine crumbs. Add butter and whiz to combine. Press evenly into the base of prepared pan. Chill in fridge until needed.

Place the cream cheese in a food processor and whiz until smooth. Add the sugar, corn flour and eggs, and whiz until combined. Add malted milk powder and whiz to combine.

Pour over biscuit base. Place cake on a baking tray and bake for 1 hour or until just set with a slight wobble in the centre. Turn off oven.

Cool cake in oven with door slightly ajar for 2 hours. Chill for at least 4 hours or overnight until cold and firm.

For the meringue, place sugar, cream of tartar and eggwhite in a heatproof bowl set over a saucepan of gently simmering water (don't let bowl touch the water), stirring until the sugar has dissolved.

Transfer to a stand mixer and whisk on high speed for 8 minutes or until stiff peaks form and meringue has cooled.

Spoon the meringue onto cheesecake, then use a kitchen blowtorch to caramelise the top of meringue just before serving.

Olive Oil Cake

8 servings

1¼ cups plus 2 tablespoons extra-virgin olive oil; plus more for pan

1 cup plus 2 tablespoons sugar; plus more

2 cups cake flour

⅓ cup almond flour or meal or fine-grind cornmeal

2 teaspoons baking powder

½ teaspoon baking soda

½ teaspoon kosher salt

3 tablespoons amaretto, Grand Marnier, sweet vermouth, or other liqueur

1 tablespoon finely grated lemon zest

3 tablespoons fresh lemon juice

2 teaspoons vanilla extract

3 large eggs

Special Equipment

A 9"-diameter springform pan

Preparation

Preheat oven to 400°. Drizzle bottom and sides of pan with oil and use your fingers to coat. Line bottom with a round of parchment paper and smooth to eliminate air

56

bubbles; coat parchment with more oil. Generously sprinkle pan with sugar and tilt to coat in an even layer; tap out excess. Whisk cake flour, almond flour, baking powder, baking soda, and salt in a medium bowl to combine and eliminate any lumps. Stir together amaretto, lemon juice, and vanilla in a small bowl.

Using an electric mixer on high speed (use whisk attachment if working with a stand mixer), beat eggs, lemon zest, and 1 cup plus 2 Tbsp. sugar in a large bowl until mixture is very light, thick, pale, and falls off the whisk or beaters in a slowly dissolving ribbon, about 3 minutes if using a stand mixer and about 5 minutes if using a hand mixer. With mixer still on high speed, gradually stream in 1¼ cups oil and beat until incorporated and mixture is even thicker. Reduce mixer speed to low and add dry ingredients in 3 additions, alternating with amaretto mixture in 2 additions, beginning and ending with dry ingredients. Fold batter several times with a large rubber spatula, making sure to scrape the bottom and sides of bowl. Scrape batter into prepared pan, smooth top, and sprinkle with more sugar.

Place cake in oven and immediately reduce oven temperature to 350°. Bake until top is golden brown, center is firm to the touch, and a tester inserted into the center comes out clean, 40–50 minutes. Transfer pan to a wire rack and let cake cool in pan 15 minutes.

Poke holes all over top of cake with a toothpick or skewer and drizzle with remaining 2 Tbsp. oil; let it absorb. Run a thin knife around edges of cake and remove ring from pan. Slide cake onto rack and let cool completely. For the best flavor and texture, wrap cake in plastic and let sit at room temperature at least a day before serving.

Do Ahead: Cake can be baked 4 days ahead. Store tightly wrapped at room temperature.

Molten Caramel Cakes

Everybody has heard of molten chocolate cake, so I thought I'd try to create a caramel version, with a toffee-ish tender cake encasing a runny dulce de leche center. Well, folks, it worked.

Makes 4

FILLING

¼ cup store-bought dulce de leche

1 tbsp. unsalted butter, room temperature

CAKES AND ASSEMBLY

⅔ cup all-purpose flour

1 tsp. kosher salt

¼ tsp. baking powder

6 tbsp. unsalted butter, plus more for ramekins, room temperature

⅓ cup sugar, plus more for ramekins

¼ cup store-bought dulce de leche

2 large eggs, room temperature

½ tsp. vanilla extract

Preparation

FILLING

Stir dulce de leche and butter in a small bowl until well combined. Dollop in 4 equal-size blobs on a metal baking dish or baking sheet. Freeze at least 30 minutes or up to overnight until very firm (the sugar will keep it from freezing completely solid).

CAKES AND ASSEMBLY

Preheat oven to 350°. Whisk flour, salt, and baking powder in a small bowl; set aside.

Coat ramekins with butter in a thin, even layer, then coat with sugar, knocking out any excess.

Using an electric mixer on medium-high speed (use the paddle attachment if you're using a stand mixer), beat ⅓ cup sugar and 6 Tbsp. butter in a medium bowl until light and fluffy, about 4 minutes. Add dulce de leche and continue to beat until incorporated, about 1 minute. Beat in eggs, one at a time, until combined, followed by vanilla. Beat mixture on medium-high speed 1 minute (it might look slightly grainy and separated, and that's okay!). Reduce mixer speed to low and beat in reserved dry ingredients until smooth.

Divide batter among prepared ramekins. Make a small divot with a spoon in the top of each mound of batter. Place frozen filling onto divots, but do not press down into batter; you want the filling cradled by the batter but still on the surface, as it will sink to the center during baking. Place ramekins on a small rimmed baking sheet. Bake cakes until tops are browned, firm to the touch (be careful when checking as the filling may ooze out and it is very hot), and a tester inserted into the cakes, avoiding the liquid centers, comes out clean, 23–25 minutes.

Invert cakes onto plates to serve. (If you invert the first cake and see slightly underdone batter—it will be tan against the filling's dark brown color—keep remaining cakes in ramekins a couple minutes longer before unmolding. You can still eat the underdone one!)

Sour Cream Coffee Cake

10 servings

1 cup (2 sticks) unsalted butter, room temperature, plus more for pan

2 cups all-purpose flour, plus more for pan

1 tbsp. baking powder

¼ tsp. kosher salt

1½ cups shelled pecans, coarsely chopped

1 tbsp. ground cinnamon

2½ cups sugar, divided

2 large eggs, beaten to blend

2 cups sour cream

1 tbsp. vanilla extract

Preparation

Place a rack in middle of oven; preheat to 350°. Butter and flour Bundt pan. Sift baking powder, salt, and 2 cups flour into a medium bowl.

Mix pecans, cinnamon, and ½ cup sugar in another medium bowl.

Using an electric mixer on medium-high speed, beat remaining 2 cups sugar and 1 cup butter in a large bowl until incorporated and smooth. Add eggs, beating well to combine and scraping down bowl, then beat in sour cream and vanilla.

Reduce mixer speed to low and beat flour mixture into butter mixture, increasing speed to medium-low if needed, until just blended. Do not overbeat.

Scrape half of batter into prepared pan. Sprinkle evenly with half of pecan mixture. Spread remaining batter over; smooth top, then sprinkle with remaining pecan mixture.

Bake cake until a tester inserted into the center comes out clean, 50–55 minutes. Let cool 20–30 minutes. Invert onto a platter and serve warm.

Heartbeet Chocolate Cake

Earthy-sweet beet purée gives this gluten-free chocolate cake a red velvet hue but also lends so much buttery moistness that you'd never guess the cake is dairy-free as well.

8–10 servings

CAKE

4 medium beets, scrubbed

2 tbsp. virgin coconut oil, plus more for pan

½ cup Dutch-process cocoa powder, plus more for pan

1½ cups almond flour

½ tsp. baking soda

½ tsp. ground cinnamon

2 oz. bittersweet chocolate, coarsely chopped

1 tsp. apple cider vinegar or distilled white vinegar

1 tsp. vanilla extract

4 large eggs

1¼ cups (packed) light brown sugar

1 tsp. kosher salt

GLAZE

4 oz. bittersweet chocolate, coarsely chopped

1 tbsp. virgin coconut oil

¼ tsp. vanilla extract

Pinch of kosher salt

Gold luster dust (for serving; optional)

Preparation

CAKE

Cook beets in a medium pot of boiling unsalted water until tender, 30–40 minutes, depending on size. Drain and rinse under cold water until cool enough to handle.

61

Cut off stem end, then peel and cut beets into large pieces. Transfer to a blender and add 2 Tbsp. water. Blend, adding water 1 Tbsp. at a time as needed, until a smooth purée forms—it should be the consistency of applesauce. Measure out 1 cup purée (reserve remaining purée for another use, such as blending into a smoothie).

Preheat oven to 350°. Line bottom of an 8" round cake pan with parchment. Grease with oil, then dust with cocoa powder, tapping out excess.

Whisk almond flour, baking soda, cinnamon, and remaining ½ cup cocoa powder in a medium bowl; set aside.

Heat chocolate and remaining 2 Tbsp. oil in a medium heatproof bowl set over a saucepan of barely simmering water, stirring often, until melted. Remove bowl from heat. Stir in vinegar, vanilla, and reserved 1 cup beet purée until smooth.

Beat eggs, brown sugar, and salt in the large bowl of a stand mixer fitted with the whisk attachment on medium-high speed (or use an electric mixer and large bowl) until more than tripled in volume and mixture holds a ribbon for several seconds when beater is lifted above batter, 5–7 minutes. Thoroughly beating the eggs is key to creating an aerated, light crumb and is a critical step when using gluten-free ingredients.

Pour chocolate-beet mixture into egg mixture and beat on medium-low speed until combined. Turn mixer off and gently tip in reserved dry ingredients. Beat on lowest speed, scraping down bowl as needed, until combined.

Transfer batter to prepared pan. Bake cake until a tester inserted into the center comes out clean and the top springs back when gently pressed, 45–50 minutes. Let cool 10 minutes. Carefully run a knife around edges of pan, then invert cake onto a wire rack and let cool.

GLAZE

Heat chocolate, oil, vanilla, and salt in a medium heatproof bowl set over a saucepan of barely simmering water, stirring often, until chocolate is melted. Let cool, stirring occasionally, until mixture is thickened and cool enough to touch, 10–15 minutes.

Place rack with cake on a rimmed baking sheet. Pour glaze over center of cake to cover top, tilting baking sheet slightly to encourage a few drips to run over sides of cake. Sprinkle with luster dust (if using). Let sit at room temperature until glaze is set, 2–3 hours.

Do Ahead: Cake (without luster dust) can be glazed 2 days ahead. Cover and store at room temperature.

Sticky Toffee Date Cake

8 servings

CAKE

Nonstick vegetable oil spray

2 cups all-purpose flour, plus more for pan

1½ cups (packed) dark brown sugar

1½ tsp. baking powder

1 tsp. ground cinnamon

1 tsp. kosher salt

½ tsp. baking soda

1 cup (2 sticks) unsalted butter, cut into pieces, room temperature

1 cup sour cream

1 tsp. vanilla extract

3 large eggs

6 oz. Medjool dates, pitted, coarsely chopped

SALTED TOFFEE SAUCE AND ASSEMBLY

¾ cup (packed) dark brown sugar

½ cup (1 stick) unsalted butter

1 tsp. vanilla extract

¾ cup sour cream, plus more for serving

1½ tsp. flaky sea salt, plus more

2 oz. Medjool dates, pitted, torn

Preparation

CAKE

Place a rack in the middle of oven; preheat to 350°. Coat Bundt pan with nonstick spray, then lightly dust with flour, tapping out excess.

Beat brown sugar, baking powder, cinnamon, salt, baking soda, and 2 cups flour in the large bowl of a stand mixer fitted with the paddle attachment on low speed until combined (or use a hand mixer and large bowl). Add butter (make sure it's at room temperature) and beat on medium-low speed until mixture resembles coarse sand. Add sour cream and vanilla and continue to beat, increasing speed from medium-low to medium as the ingredients begin to incorporate, until batter is thick and smooth, about 1 minute. Scrape down sides of bowl. Reduce mixer speed to medium-low, add 1 egg, then increase speed to medium and beat 30 seconds. Repeat with remaining 2 eggs, reducing speed to medium-low after each addition, then increasing speed to medium-high and beating for 30 seconds (if you beat on medium-high speed from the get-go, you risk losing some of the batter; this ensures nothing flies out of the bowl). Scrape down sides of bowl again. Reduce speed to low, add dates, and beat until incorporated, about 30 seconds longer.

Scrape batter into prepared pan; smooth surface. Bake cake until a tester inserted into the center comes out clean and cake springs back slightly when pressed, 40–50 minutes. Let cool at least 20 minutes in pan, then turn out cake onto a platter and let cool completely.

Do Ahead: Cake can be made 1 day ahead. Let cool, then cover with plastic wrap. Store at room temperature.

SALTED TOFFEE SAUCE AND ASSEMBLY

Melt brown sugar and butter in a small saucepan over medium-low heat, whisking constantly, until mixture is thick and smooth and brown sugar is dissolved, 4–6 minutes. Remove pot from heat and whisk in vanilla, ¾ cup sour cream, and 1½ tsp. sea salt until smooth.

Arrange torn dates in a ring on top of cake. Drizzle ½ cup sauce over cake and dates. Sprinkle with more sea salt. Serve cake with sour cream and remaining toffee sauce alongside. If the sauce has cooled and tightened up, gently reheat in saucepan over medium-low just until warm.

Kouign-Amann

Though the dough can be temperamental, layer after delicate layer will convince you: Making this pastry is worth the effort.

12 Servings

DOUGH

2 tablespoons (30 g) European-style butter (at least 82% fat), melted, slightly cooled, plus more for bowl

1 tablespoon (10 g) active dry yeast

3 tablespoons (40 g) sugar

1 teaspoon (5 g) kosher salt

3 cups (400 g) all-purpose flour, plus more for surface

BUTTER BLOCK

12 oz. (340 g) chilled unsalted European-style butter (at least 82% fat), cut into pieces

½ cup (100 g) sugar

1 teaspoon (5 g) kosher salt

ASSEMBLY

All-purpose flour

¾ cup (150 g) sugar, divided

Nonstick vegetable oil spray

SPECIAL EQUIPMENT:

Two 6-cup jumbo muffin pans; ruler

Preparation

DOUGH

Brush a large bowl with butter. Whisk yeast and ¼ cup very warm water (110°–115°) in another large bowl to dissolve. Let stand until yeast starts to foam, about 5 minutes. Add sugar, salt, 3 cups flour, 2 Tbsp. butter, and ¾ cup cold water. Mix until a shaggy dough forms. Turn out onto a lightly floured surface and knead, adding flour as needed, until dough is supple, soft, and slightly tacky, about 5 minutes.

Place dough in prepared bowl and turn to coat with butter. Cover bowl with plastic wrap, place in a warm, draft-free spot, and let dough rise until doubled in size, 1–1½ hours. (This process of resting and rising is known as proofing.) Punch down dough and knead lightly a few times inside bowl. Cover again with plastic wrap and chill in refrigerator until dough is again doubled in size, 45–60 minutes.

Turn out dough onto a lightly floured surface and pat into a 6x6" square. Wrap in plastic and chill in freezer until dough is very firm but not frozen, 30–35 minutes. (Heads up: You'll want it to be about as firm as the chilled butter block.)

BUTTER BLOCK

Beat butter, sugar, and salt with an electric mixer on low speed just until homogeneous and waxy-looking, about 3 minutes. Scrape butter mixture onto a large sheet of parchment. Shape into a 12x6" rectangle ¼" thick.

Neatly wrap up butter, pressing out air. Roll packet gently with a rolling pin to push butter into corners and create an evenly thick rectangle. Chill in refrigerator until firm but pliable, 25–30 minutes.

ASSEMBLY

Roll out dough on a lightly floured surface into a 19x7" rectangle (a bit wider and about 50 percent longer than the butter block). Place butter block on upper two-thirds of dough, leaving a thin border along top and sides. Fold dough like a letter: Bring lower third of dough up and over lower half of butter. Then fold exposed upper half of butter and dough over lower half (butter should bend, not break). Press edges of dough to seal, enclosing butter.

Rotate dough package 90° counterclockwise so flap opening is on your right. Roll out dough, dusting with flour as needed, to a 24x8" rectangle about ⅜" thick.

Fold rectangle into thirds like a letter (same as before), bringing lower third up, then upper third down (this completes the first turn).

Dust dough lightly with flour, wrap in plastic, and chill in freezer until firm but not frozen, about 30 minutes. Transfer to refrigerator; continue to chill until very firm, about 1 hour longer. (Freezing dough first cuts down on chilling time.)

Place dough on surface so flap opening is on your right. Roll out dough, dusting with flour as needed, to a 24x8" rectangle, about ⅜" thick. Fold into thirds (same way as before), rotate 90° counterclockwise so flap opening is on your right, and roll out again to a 24x8" rectangle.

Sprinkle surface of dough with 2 Tbsp. sugar; fold into thirds. Dust lightly with flour, wrap in plastic, and chill in freezer until firm but not frozen, about 30 minutes. Transfer to refrigerator; continue to chill until very firm, about 1 hour longer.

Place dough on surface so flap opening is on your right. Roll out dough, dusting with flour as needed, to a rectangle slightly larger than 16x12". Trim to 16x12". Cut into 12 squares (you'll want a 4x3 grid). Brush excess flour from dough and surface.

Lightly coat muffin cups with nonstick spray. Sprinkle squares with a total of ¼ cup sugar, dividing evenly, and press gently to adhere. Turn over and repeat with another ¼ cup sugar, pressing gently to adhere. Shake off excess. Lift corners of each square and press into the center. Place each in a muffin cup. Wrap pans with plastic and chill in refrigerator at least 8 hours and up to 12 hours (dough will be puffed with slightly separated layers).

Preheat oven to 375°. Unwrap pans and sprinkle kouign-amann with remaining 2 Tbsp. sugar, dividing evenly. Bake until pastry is golden brown all over and sugar is deeply caramelized, 25–30 minutes (make sure to bake pastries while dough is still cold). Immediately remove from pan and transfer to a wire rack; let cool.

6.

ROLLS, BUNS AND DOUGHNUTS

Cinnamon-Date Buns

Makes 16 Servings

DATE FILLING

16 Medjool dates, pitted (about 8 oz.)

¼ teaspoon kosher salt

½ cup (1 stick) unsalted butter, room temperature

1 tablespoon finely grated orange zest

1 teaspoon ground cinnamon

DOUGH AND ASSEMBLY

⅓ cup whole milk

4 tablespoons honey, divided

1 envelope active dry yeast (about 2¼ tsp.)

2 large egg yolks

2 large eggs

⅓ cup buttermilk

1 cup spelt flour

1¼ teaspoon kosher salt

2 cups all-purpose flour, plus more for surface

½ cup (1 stick) unsalted butter, cut into pieces, room temperature, plus melted butter for bowl and brushing

¼ cup sugar

1 teaspoon ground cinnamon

Preparation

DATE FILLING

Bring dates, salt, and 1½ cups water to a boil in a medium saucepan. Reduce heat and simmer, stirring and mashing occasionally, until dates are falling apart and water is evaporated (it should be a thick paste), 10–15 minutes. Let cool, then stir in butter, orange zest, and cinnamon.

DO AHEAD: Date filling can be made 1 week ahead. Cover and chill. Bring to room temperature before using.

DOUGH AND ASSEMBLY

Preheat oven to 375°. Heat milk and 1 Tbsp. honey in a small saucepan until lukewarm. Combine milk mixture and yeast in the bowl of a stand mixer. As soon as yeast is foamy, about 5 minutes, add egg yolks, 1 egg, buttermilk, spelt flour, salt, 2 cups all-purpose flour, and remaining 3 Tbsp. honey; mix on medium speed until dough is smooth, shiny, and elastic, 5–8 minutes.

With motor running, add ½ cup room-temperature butter, 1 piece at a time, waiting until each piece is incorporated before adding the next. Mix 1 minute, then increase speed to medium-high and mix until dough is soft and supple, 6–8 minutes. (No stand mixer? Whisk ingredients into yeast mixture in a large bowl, then knead dough on a clean surface. Mix in butter with a sturdy wooden spoon, then knead briefly to make sure butter is well incorporated.)

Place dough in a buttered medium bowl. Brush with melted butter; cover with plastic wrap. Let dough rise in a warm spot until doubled in size, 1–1½ hours (2–2½ hours if dough was made ahead and chilled).

Divide dough in half. Roll out 1 piece on a lightly floured surface to a 15x5" rectangle. Evenly spread with half of date filling and cut into 8 triangles. Starting with a pointy end, roll up dough (like a reverse crescent roll). Place, seam side down, on a parchment-lined baking sheet. Repeat with remaining dough, date filling, and another baking sheet.

Cover buns with plastic wrap and let rise in a warm spot until almost doubled in size, 30–40 minutes.

Mix sugar and cinnamon in a small bowl. Whisk remaining egg and 1 tsp. water in another small bowl and brush over buns. Sprinkle with cinnamon sugar; bake until golden brown, 20–25 minutes. Let cool slightly before serving.

DO AHEAD: Dough (before rise) can be made 1 day ahead. Cover and chill.

Miso Doughnuts

You'll make use of all those fancy attachments with this recipe.

Makes about 30 Servings

2 teaspoons red miso

¾ cup plus 1 tablespoon sugar, divided

1 ¼-ounce envelope active dry yeast (about 2¼ teaspoons)

1 large egg, room temperature

1 large egg yolk, room temperature

3 tablespoons unsalted butter, melted

3 tablespoons whole milk, room temperature

3 tablespoons white miso

1 cup bread flour

1 cup all-purpose flour, plus more for dusting

Nonstick vegetable oil spray

Vegetable oil (for frying; about 8 cups)

SPECIAL EQUIPMENT

1½ diameter biscuit cutter; a deep-fry thermometer

Preparation

Pulse red miso and ½ cup sugar in a food processor until mixture resembles brown sugar. Spread out evenly on a parchment-lined rimmed baking sheet and let sit until dry, 2–2 ½ hours. Pulse in food processor until no clumps remain. Transfer miso sugar to a medium bowl.

Combine 1 Tbsp. sugar and ¼ cup warm water in a small bowl. Sprinkle yeast over and let sit until foamy, 5–10 minutes.

Beat egg, egg yolk, butter, milk, white miso, and remaining ¼ cup sugar in the bowl of a stand mixer fitted with whisk attachment (or use a whisk and a medium bowl) until miso breaks up into small pieces and mixture is almost smooth. Add yeast mixture along with bread flour and 1 cup all-purpose flour and mix until a shaggy ball forms (or, use a sturdy wooden spoon and some effort).

Switch to dough hook and mix on medium until dough is soft, smooth, elastic, and climbing up hook, 5–7 minutes. (Or, knead on a lightly floured surface, 8–10 minutes.) If dough is wet, add more all-purpose flour as needed.

Place dough in a large bowl lightly coated with nonstick spray. Cover and let sit in a warm place until nearly doubled in size, 1–2 hours.

Line a baking sheet with parchment paper; lightly flour. Turn out dough onto a lightly floured surface and pat out to 1" thick. Punch out rounds with biscuit cutter. Repeat with scraps. Transfer rounds to prepared baking sheet, cover loosely, and let rise in a warm place until almost doubled in size, 45–60 minutes.

Pour oil into a large heavy saucepan to a depth of 2". Heat over medium-high until thermometer registers 325°. Working in batches, fry doughnuts until deep golden brown, about 3 minutes per side. Transfer to paper towels and let cool slightly before tossing in miso sugar.

Do Ahead: Dough (before rise) can be made 1 day ahead; cover and chill.

Glazed Cinnamon-Cardamom Buns

Active Time 1 hour 10 minutes

Total Time 5 hours 20 minutes, plus an overnight proof

Makes 8

For the Dough:

1 cup whole milk

1 Tbsp. active dry yeast

1 large egg

1 large egg yolk

3 1/2 cups (475 g) all-purpose flour

1/2 cup (105 g) granulated sugar

1 1/2 tsp. (3 g) ground cardamom

1 tsp. kosher salt

6 Tbsp. room temperature unsalted butter, plus more for bowl

For the Filling and Assembly:

6 Tbsp. unsalted butter, room temperature

3 Tbsp. ground cinnamon

1 1/2 cups (packed) brown sugar, divided

All-purpose flour (for surface)

For the Dough:

Heat milk in a small saucepan over low until just warm; an instant-read thermometer should register 105°F–115°F. Pour into the large bowl of a stand mixer. Whisk in yeast and let sit until foamy, 10–15 minutes. You should see a layer of foam on the surface; this means that the yeast is active.

Add egg, egg yolk, flour, granulated sugar, cardamom, and salt to yeast mixture and mix with dough hook on low speed until well combined. Increase speed to medium and continue to mix until dough is smooth and elastic, about 10 minutes. Gradually add butter 1 Tbsp. at a time, mixing to incorporate slightly before adding more. When 6 Tbsp. butter are incorporated, mix until dough is smooth, supple, and shiny, 10–15 minutes longer (you need to mix this long to develop the gluten).

Transfer dough to a large buttered bowl, cover with plastic wrap and a kitchen towel, and let sit at room temperature until doubled in size, 1–1 1/2 hours. Punch dough down, cover bowl tightly in plastic wrap, and chill overnight (the slow proof creates more flavor because it gives the yeast more time to process the sugar).

For the Filling and Assembly:

Mix butter, cinnamon, and 1/2 cup brown sugar in a medium bowl until combined.

Have your tools and filling nearby; you want to work quickly and keep dough as chilled as possible to make rolling more manageable. Turn out dough onto a lightly floured piece of parchment paper and roll to a 1/4"-thick rectangle, about 16"x12". Cover with plastic and chill until dough is firm, 30–60 minutes.

Spread butter mixture over two-thirds of dough. Fold plain side over the middle, then fold opposite third over (like folding an envelope). Roll to a 12"x8" rectangle about 1/2" thick. Slice lengthwise into eight 1"-thick strips.

Working one at a time, lay strip on clean work surface with long side facing you. Using your palms, gently twist each end in opposite directions until entire strip is spiraled. Hold one end of strip between a thumb and index finger. Working away from you, tightly wrap strip around 3 fingers. Wrap around fingers again, placing second loop closer to the palm of your hand. As you bring strip across the back of your hand, cross over first loop, angling toward the end of your index finger. Cross dough over front of your hand and tuck the end into the center while removing your fingers and pushing through to the other side to create a knot. Check out step-by-step photos here. You want to twist these tightly so that they rise while baking. If you're having trouble, twist them into any kind of knot that you can—just make sure it's wrapped tightly.

Divide cinnamon twists between 2 rimmed baking sheets, spacing evenly apart. Cover loosely with plastic wrap and let sit at room temperature until doubled in size, 45–60 minutes.

Place racks in upper and lower thirds of oven; preheat to 325°F. Bake cinnamon buns, rotating pans from top to bottom halfway through, until deeply golden brown, 25–30 minutes.

Bring remaining 1 cup brown sugar and 1/2 cup water to a boil in a small saucepan. Generously brush syrup over hot buns. If you like a sweeter pastry, wait 5 minutes, then brush again.

Orange Sweet Rolls

Active Time 1 hour, 10 minutes

Total Time 2 hours, 40 minutes

Makes 12

For the filling:

1/2 cup (1 stick) unsalted butter, softened

1/2 cup sugar

1 tablespoon finely grated orange zest

1/8 teaspoon kosher salt

Pinch of ground cardamom (optional)

For the rolls:

1 (1/4-ounce) envelope active dry yeast (about 2 1/4 teaspoons)

2 tablespoons sugar, divided

1 egg yolk, lightly beaten, room temperature

1/3 cup fresh orange juice

2 tablespoons melted coconut oil, cooled, or vegetable shortening

1/2 teaspoon kosher salt

1 2/3 cup cups all-purpose flour, plus more for surface

Nonstick vegetable oil spray

Special Equipment:

A 12-cup standard muffin tin

Make the filling:

Using an electric mixer on medium-high speed, beat butter, sugar, orange zest, salt, and cardamom, if using, in a large bowl until fluffy.

Make and assemble the rolls:

Pour 3 Tbsp. warm water (105°F–115°F) into a small bowl. Add yeast and 1 Tbsp. sugar and whisk to combine. Let sit until foamy, about 10 minutes.

Using electric mixer on medium-high speed, beat egg yolk, orange juice, oil, salt, and remaining 1 Tbsp. sugar in a large bowl. Add 1 2/3 cups flour and yeast mixture. Beat until dough just comes together. Turn out dough onto a lightly floured surface. Knead several times with floured hands until smooth, about 5 minutes (dough will be sticky).

Spray a clean large bowl with nonstick spray. Place dough in bowl and turn to coat. Cover with a towel and let sit in a warm place until doubled in size, about 45 minutes.

Spray muffin tin with nonstick spray. Roll dough on a well floured surface to an 1/8"-thick rectangle about 17x14". Spread filling over dough, leaving a 1/2" border on all sides. Starting on 1 long side, roll dough into a tight cylinder. Cut into 12 equal pieces (if it's difficult to cut, chill 15 minutes). Transfer cut side up to prepared muffin tin. Cover with a towel and let sit in a warm, draft-free place until risen, 30 minutes, or chill overnight. If chilling, let sit at room temperature 2 hours to rise before baking.

Preheat oven to 350°F. Bake rolls, rotating pans halfway through, until lightly browned on top, 15–18 minutes. Let cool in pan 5 minutes, then invert onto a platter to serve.

Pull-Apart Potato Rolls

These super-soft rolls are great for parties because you can just plunk down the pan in front of your guests and let them have at it.

Makes 18 Servings

1 medium Yukon Gold potato (about 6 ounces), scrubbed

1 cup whole milk

½ cup (1 stick) unsalted butter, melted, plus more for brushing

1½ cups all-purpose flour

2 ¼-ounce envelopes active dry yeast (about 4½ teaspoons)

3 (heaping) tablespoons sugar

2 large eggs, beaten to blend

1 large egg yolk, beaten to blend

2⅔ cups (or more) bread flour

1 tablespoon flaky sea salt, plus more

Vegetable oil (for surface)

SPECIAL EQUIPMENT

A potato ricer

Preparation

Boil potato in a small saucepan of boiling water (no need to add salt) until a paring knife passes through flesh with no resistance, 30–40 minutes; drain. When cool enough to handle, pass through ricer into a small bowl (peel won't go through; discard).

Mix milk and ¾ cup riced potato in the bowl of a stand mixer with whisk attachment until no lumps remain. Add ½ cup butter and mix until incorporated. Switch to dough hook. Add all-purpose flour, yeast, and sugar and mix on medium speed, scraping bottom and sides of bowl as needed, until a very wet, sticky dough forms, about 2 minutes.

Let dough rise, uncovered, in a warm spot, 30 minutes (it will have puffed slightly).

Add eggs, egg yolk, 2⅔ cups bread flour, and 1 Tbsp. salt and mix on medium-high, adding more bread flour if needed, until dough is smooth and elastic, about 5 minutes. Brush surface of dough with butter, cover, and let rise in a warm spot 30 minutes (dough should rise 1½ times its initial size).

Turn out dough onto a lightly oiled surface and divide into 18 pieces; roll each into a ball using your palm. Brush a 13x9" baking dish with butter and place balls side by side in dish (rolls will be touching). Brush tops with more butter. Let sit, uncovered, in a warm spot 1 hour.

Preheat oven to 400°. Brush dough again with butter and sprinkle with salt. Bake rolls until deep golden brown, 15–20 minutes. Transfer dish to a wire rack and let rolls cool in dish 10 minutes. Turn out rolls onto rack and let cool 30 minutes before serving.

Coffee-Glazed Doughnuts

Active Time 45 min Total Time 3 3/4 hr

Makes about 1 dozen doughnuts

For doughnuts

1 (1/4-oz) package active dry yeast (2 1/2 teaspoons)

2 tablespoons warm water (105–115°F)

3 1/4 cups all-purpose flour plus additional for sprinkling and rolling out dough

1 cup whole milk at room temperature

1/2 stick (1/4 cup) unsalted butter, softened

3 large egg yolks

2 tablespoons sugar

1 1/2 teaspoons salt

1/2 teaspoon cinnamon

About 10 cups vegetable oil for deep frying

For glaze

1/4 cup boiling-hot water

5 teaspoons instant-espresso powder or instant-coffee granules

1 1/2 cups confectioners sugar

1 tablespoon light corn syrup

1/4 teaspoon pure vanilla extract

1/4 teaspoon salt

About 1/4 cup sanding sugar (optional)

Special Equipment:

a stand mixer fitted with paddle attachment; a 3-inch and a 1-inch round cookie cutter; a deep-fat thermometer

Make dough:

Stir together yeast and warm water in a small bowl until yeast is dissolved. Let stand until foamy, about 5 minutes. (If yeast doesn't foam, discard and start over with new yeast.)

Mix together flour, milk, butter, yolks, sugar, salt, cinnamon, and yeast mixture in mixer at low speed until a soft dough forms. Increase speed to medium-high and beat 3 minutes more.

Scrape dough down side of bowl (all around) into center, then sprinkle lightly with flour (to keep a crust from forming). Cover bowl with a clean kitchen towel (not terry cloth) and let dough rise in a draft-free place at warm room temperature until doubled in bulk, 1 1/2 to 2 hours. (Alternatively, let dough rise in bowl in refrigerator 8 to 12 hours.)

Turn dough out onto a lightly floured surface and roll out with a lightly floured rolling pin into a 12-inch round (1/2 inch thick). Cut out as many rounds as possible with 3-inch cutter, then cut a hole in center of each round with 1-inch cutter and transfer doughnuts to a lightly floured large baking sheet. Cover doughnuts with a clean kitchen towel and let rise in a draft-free place at warm room temperature until slightly puffed, about 30 minutes (45 minutes if dough was cold when cutting out doughnuts). Do not reroll scraps.

Heat 2 1/2 inches oil in a deep 4-quart heavy pot until it registers 350°F on thermometer. Fry doughnuts, 2 at a time, turning occasionally with a wire or mesh skimmer or a slotted spoon, until puffed and golden brown, about 2 minutes per batch. Transfer to paper towels to drain. (Return oil to 350°F between batches.)

Make glaze:

Stir together boiling-hot water and espresso powder in a medium bowl until powder is dissolved, then stir in confectioners sugar, corn syrup, vanilla, and salt until smooth.

Dip doughnuts into glaze, turning to coat well, then put on a rack set in a shallow baking pan (to catch any drips). While glaze is wet, sprinkle doughnuts with sanding sugar (if using). Let stand until glaze is set, about 20 minutes.

7. DESSERTS

Berry Pavlovas

Makes about 12 Servings

MERINGUE

1¼ cups sugar

6 large egg whites

Pinch of cream of tartar

½ teaspoon kosher salt

1 vanilla bean, split lengthwise, or 2 teaspoons vanilla extract

¾ cup chopped almonds, walnuts, or pistachios, and/or 3 tablespoons poppy seeds

ASSEMBLY

¼ cup sugar

36 ounces raspberries and/or blackberries (about 6 cups), divided

1¼ cups heavy cream

Preparation

MERINGUE

Preheat oven to 350°. Scatter sugar in a shallow baking dish and bake 10 minutes. After 8 minutes, using an electric mixer on medium-high speed, beat egg whites and cream of tartar in a large bowl until foamy.

Remove sugar from oven and decrease temperature to 200°. With the mixer running, gradually stream sugar into egg whites. Add salt and beat until stiff peaks form and bowl is barely warm to the touch. (Heads up: This can take as much as 10 minutes with a stand mixer and up to 20 minutes with a handheld mixer.) Scrape in vanilla seeds, reserve pod for another use, and beat just to combine.

Scoop large spoonfuls of meringue onto 2 parchment-lined baking sheets to make 12 mounds. Make a slight indentation in the center of each mound with the back of the spoon, pushing out to create 3"-diameter rounds. Top the border of meringues with nuts and/or poppy seeds, as desired.

Bake meringues until dry and firm, about 2 hours and 15 minutes. Turn off oven and use a wooden spoon to prop door ajar. Let meringues cool completely in oven.

Do Ahead: Meringues can be made 1 day ahead. Store tightly wrapped at room temperature.

ASSEMBLY

Combine sugar and 2 cups berries in a medium bowl and mash together with a fork until sugar is dissolved and mixture is bright in color and pourable.

Whisk cream in a medium bowl to medium peaks. Spoon whipped cream into centers of meringues, top with remaining berries, then drizzle with sauce.

Do Ahead: Berry sauce can be made 4 hours ahead. Store tightly covered at room temperature.

Hamantaschen

Makes about 24 Servings

4 cups (500 g) all-purpose flour, plus more for surface

1½ teaspoons baking powder

1 cup (2 sticks) unsalted butter, room temperature

1 cup (200 g) sugar

1 teaspoon kosher salt

1 tsp. (packed) finely grated lemon zest

2 large eggs, room temperature

Date-Orange Filling, Honey-Nut Filling, Poppy Seed Filling, or 1½ cups jam or preserves

SPECIAL EQUIPMENT

3½ "-diameter cookie cutter

Preparation

Whisk 4 cups (500g) all-purpose flour, and 1 ½ tsp. baking powder in small bowl until well combined.

Beat 1 cup (2 sticks) unsalted butter, 1 cup (200g) sugar, 1 tsp. Diamond Crystal kosher salt, and 1 tsp. (packed) finely grated lemon zest in a stand mixer fitted with paddle attachment on medium speed until pale and creamy, about 3 minutes. Add 2 large eggs, one at a time, beating for 30 seconds after each addition and scraping down sides of bowl. Reduce speed to low and add dry ingredients; beat until just combined. Divide dough in half and pat into disks.

Working one disk at a time, roll out dough between 2 sheets of parchment paper to ¼" thick. Stack sheets of dough, still sandwiched between parchment, and slide onto a baking sheet. Chill until firm, about 1 hour.

Roll out dough on a very lightly floured surface to about ¼" thick, dusting with flour as needed (use as little flour as possible). Cut out 3 1/2" rounds with cutter and, using an offset spatula or bench scraper, transfer to 2 parchment-lined baking sheets. Gather up scraps, reroll, and cut out additional rounds.

Place racks in upper and lower thirds of oven; preheat to 350°. Unstack dough sheets and transfer to a surface; carefully peel away top sheet of parchment paper from each. Punch out cookies as close together as possible with cutter. Transfer cutouts to 2 parchment-lined baking sheets (reuse the top sheets from rolling out cookies). Gather up scraps, reroll, and cut out additional rounds, chilling dough briefly in between if needed.

Place 2 tsp. of your chosen filling in center of each cookie round. Fold three sides up and over filling (leaving about 1" of filling exposed) to make a triangle, pressing points gently but firmly to seal.

Bake cookies, rotating baking sheets top to bottom and front to back, until bottoms are golden brown, 18-22 minutes. Let cool 5 minutes on baking sheets, then transfer to wire rack and let cool completely.

Do ahead: Dough can be rolled out 2 days ahead; stack, sandwiched between parchment, on a baking sheet, wrap in plastic, and chill. Cookies can be assembled 3 days ahead; store airtight at room temperature.

Chocolate Mousse

Prep Time: 10 mins Cook Time: 10 mins Cooling Time: 2 hrs

Total Time: 20 mins

4 egg yolks

1/4 cup granulated sugar

2 1/2 cups whipping cream, (divided)

8 ounces semi sweet baking chocolate, chopped

2 teaspoons vanilla extract

For the garnish:

shaved chocolate

whipped cream

Preparation

Beat egg yolks in the bowl of a stand mixer with the whisk attachment for 3 minutes until thick. Gradually add the sugar while beating.

Heat 1 cup of cream in a small sauce pan until hot. With the mixer on, stream 1/2 of the hot cream into the eggs. Once combined, pour the mixture into the pot with the remaining 1/2 cup cream. Turn the heat to low and cook until thick, stirring constantly (5 minutes).

Mix in the vanilla and then add in the chocolate in 3 batches, stirring over low heat until melted and smooth.

Pour the mix into a large bowl, cover, and place in fridge for 1.5-2 hours, stirring every 20-30 minutes. Once no longer warm, remove from the fridge and whip up the remaining 1 1/2 cups heavy cream to stiff peaks. Fold the cream into the cooled chocolate mixture.

Pipe or spoon the mouse into small glasses. Cover and place in fridge until ready to serve.

Garnish with fresh whipped cream and shaved chocolate.

Fresh Pasta

4 (makes 12 oz.) Servings

1 cup plus 2 tablespoons fine durum wheat flour or all-purpose flour plus more for dusting

1 cup semolina flour (pasta flour)

Ingredient Info:

Fine durum wheat flour is available at natural foods stores and some specialty foods stores. Semolina flour is available at Italian markets, specialty foods stores, and some supermarkets.

Preparation

Combine durum wheat flour and semolina flour in a large bowl. Bring a small saucepan of water to a bare simmer. Add ⅔ cup hot water to flours and mix with a fork until mixture just comes together. Turn out dough onto a surface lightly dusted with durum wheat flour and knead until smooth and elastic, 8–10 minutes (alternatively, using a stand mixer fitted with a dough hook, mix on low speed, about 5 minutes). Wrap tightly in plastic wrap; let sit 1 hour at room temperature.

Do Ahead: Pasta dough can be made a day ahead. Wrap tightly and chill.

Green Chorizo

Makes 12–14 links; about 4 lb. Servings

14-lb. skinless, boneless pork shoulder (Boston butt), cut into 1–2" pieces

6 bay leaves

1 tablespoon freshly ground black pepper

30 grams* kosher salt, plus more

6 oz. flat-leaf spinach, trimmed

10 serrano chiles, halved, seeds removed

2 teaspoons finely grated garlic

¼ cup toasted pumpkin seeds, coarsely chopped

2 tablespoons finely chopped fresh oregano

2 29–32-mm-diameter natural hog casings, preferably pretubed or preloaded

Preparation

Chill all grinder parts, including die with ¼" holes, in freezer until very cold, about 1 hour. Chill a large stainless-steel bowl in refrigerator until cold. Place pork in a single layer on 2 plastic wrap–lined baking sheets; cover and freeze until meat is very firm but not frozen, about 1 hour.

Grind bay leaves in a spice mill. Combine with black pepper and 30 grams salt in a small bowl; set aside.

Cook spinach in a pot of boiling salted water until wilted, about 15 seconds; drain and run under cold water. Drain well, squeeze out as much liquid as possible. Blend with chiles and 2 Tbsp. cold water in a blender until coarsely chopped; set aside.

Grind pork on high speed, 3–4 pieces at a time, into chilled bowl (keep second baking sheet in freezer until ready to use). If grinder clogs (meat will look pink, not red and white), clean die and cutter before continuing.

Add garlic and mix gently with your hands just to begin to distribute, about 20 seconds. Sprinkle reserved spice mixture evenly over pork and knead, rotating bowl, until spice mixture is evenly distributed and a light film has formed on the side of the bowl, about 1 minute.

Add pumpkin seeds and oregano and mix gently with your hands just to begin to distribute, about 20 seconds, then add reserved spinach mixture and knead until mixture holds together and is very stiff (it will spring back when pressed), about 1 minute. (Don't overmix or sausage will be crumbly.)

Form ¼ cup sausage mixture into a 3"-diameter patty; press into palm. Extend hand with meat, palm facing down. If meat sticks for at least 5 seconds, it is sufficiently mixed. If not, continue to knead in 15-second intervals until it passes the palm test.

Wrap patty in a small sheet of foil to form a flat packet. Cover and chill remaining mixture.

Cook foil-wrapped patty in a small skillet (not nonstick) over medium-low heat until meat is cooked through, about 4 minutes per side. Let rest 2 minutes.

Unwrap patty and cut in half; it should hold together. If not, save for another use—like pasta sauce—and try again.

Place casings in a large bowl under cold running water and let sit, allowing water to overflow and flushing water through casings (take care not to tangle!) until softened, about 2 minutes. Slide 1 casing onto stuffer nozzle, leaving a 6″ overhang (do not tie). If casing is too long or tangles, cut in half and work with 1 piece at a time.

Pack a handful of sausage mixture very lightly into stuffer. Working with a partner and with stuffer on high speed, use plunger to push meat through, gradually filling casing; gently slide filled casing off nozzle onto a baking sheet as you go.

Fill casing firmly but don't overstuff (mixture will tighten when links are twisted, and overfilled casings will burst when cooked). As casing fills, lightly prick air bubbles with sausage pricker. Leave at least 6″ of empty casing at the end. Repeat with remaining casing and sausage mixture.

Tie off 1 end of casing, making knot flush with meat. Starting 6″ from knot, pinch off a 6″ length, squeezing on both sides. Twist link toward you 2 rotations. Starting 6″ from link, pinch off another 6″ length, squeezing on both sides, and twist link away from you 2 rotations. Repeat, alternating direction of twists, until you can't make another 6″ sausage. Squeeze out extra meat; tie off casing.

Note: If casing bursts, pinch off on both sides of tear, squeeze out meat in the middle, and tie off casing. Begin again as from the start.

Prick each sausage link in 3 places with sausage pricker (this helps prevent bursting). Arrange links on a parchment-lined baking sheet and chill, uncovered, to dry out casings, at least 12 hours.

Using kitchen shears, cut casing between links to separate.

Do Ahead: Sausage mixture can be made 4 hours ahead (longer and meat will begin to cure); chill. Sausages can be made 3 days ahead. Cover and chill. Alternatively, freeze on baking sheet until frozen, then store in resealable plastic freezer bags up to 3 months. Defrost 12 hours in refrigerator before cooking.

Pretzel Bites

Makes about 64

2 tablespoons unsalted butter, cut into pieces, room temperature, plus more for greasing

1 ¼-ounce package active dry yeast (about 2¼ teaspoons)

1 tablespoon dark brown sugar

3¼ cups (or more) unbleached bread flour

½ cup cold pilsner-style beer

2 teaspoons kosher salt

¼ cup baking soda

Vegetable oil (for greasing)

1 large egg

Coarse kosher salt, pretzel salt, everything seasoning, paprika, caraway seeds, and/or poppy seeds (for topping)

Spicy Cheddar Cheese Spread and/or mustard (for serving)

Preparation

Grease a very large bowl with butter. Pour ½ cup warm water (100°–115°) into the bowl of a stand mixer. Sprinkle yeast over. Add brown sugar and stir to dissolve. Let sit until foamy, 5–7 minutes.

Stir in bread flour, beer, kosher salt, and remaining 2 Tbsp. butter with a wooden spoon or spatula until a shaggy dough forms. Mix with dough hook on medium-low speed until dough forms into a smooth ball, about 2 minutes. (You might need to help dough form into a ball by scraping up some flour from bottom of bowl with your hands.) Dough should be firm and might be a little tacky, but not sticky. If dough is still sticky, add flour 1 Tbsp. at a time, mixing until smooth. If dough is too dry, add warm water 1 tsp. at a time. Continue to mix on medium-low speed until dough is smooth and elastic, 5–7 minutes. (Alternatively, mix dough ingredients in a large bowl, then turn out onto a clean work surface and knead by hand, about 10 minutes.)

Transfer dough to prepared bowl and cover tightly with plastic wrap. Let rise in a warm place until doubled in volume, about 1½ hours.

Place racks in upper and lower thirds of oven; preheat to 500°. Turn out dough onto a clean work surface and punch down to deflate. Divide into 8 equal pieces (if you have a kitchen scale, weigh the dough before cutting, then divide by weight; otherwise, eyeball it). Working with 1 piece at a time and keeping remaining dough covered with a damp kitchen towel, shape dough into a rope about 12" long and ¾" in diameter, applying light pressure with your palms and working from center of dough out to the ends. If you need more friction, lightly spray work surface with water.

Cut rope into 8 pieces about 1½" long. Arrange on 2 rimmed baking sheets, spacing ½" apart. Repeat with remaining pieces of dough. Cover with plastic wrap and let rise at room temperature until increased in size by about half, 20–30 minutes.

While dough pieces are going through second rise, bring 8 cups water to a boil in a large pot. Carefully add baking soda, which will bubble violently.

Using a large spider and working in 2 batches, gently dip dough pieces into boiling solution. Cook, turning, until pieces are fully coated, about 20 seconds. Using spider, remove from liquid and drain on paper towels. Divide between 2 lightly oiled rimmed baking sheets, spacing at least 1" apart.

Beat egg with 1 Tbsp. water in a small bowl, then brush dough pieces with egg wash. Sprinkle with toppings. Bake pretzels, rotating sheets from front to back and top to bottom halfway through, until deep brown in color, 8–12 minutes. Let cool slightly.

Serve pretzel bites with cheese dip and/or mustard alongside.

Do Ahead: Pretzel dough before rises can be made 1 day ahead. Wrap in plastic and chill. Let come to room temperature, then let rise in a warm place until doubled in volume, 3–4 hours.

8. MAIN DISHES

Mashed Potato

Prep: 20 minutes Cook: 20 minutes

Serves 4

8 large potatoes

1 tbsp butter

4 tbsp Milk

Salt / Pepper / seasoning as required

Preparation

Peel and chop potatoes into equal-sized pieces

Add potatoes to a large pan of cold water, rinse of additional starch and drain

Boil the kettle, and add to the pan of potatoes. Place on a hob/stovetop and simmer until a fork is inserted with no resistance.

Drain the potatoes and set aside, ensuring they are dry before proceeding

Tip potatoes into your mixer and attach the flat beater

Beat the potatoes on low (speed 1-2) for 1 minute, until all visible lumps have disappeared

Switch the flat beater for your wire whisk

Whisk on high for 1-2 minutes, until smooth

Add milk and butter, and mix on medium until absorbed

Add salt/pepper, and any seasoning you'd like (chilli flakes? Garlic salt? Whatever you fancy!)

Homemade Pasta

Servings1 1/4 lbs dough

3 1/2 cups all-purpose unbleached flour, sifted (plus extra flour for preparing)

1/2 teaspoon salt

4 large eggs, beaten

2 tablespoons water

Preparation

Place eggs, water, flour and salt in mixer bowl. Attached bowl and flat beater. Turn to speed 2 and mix for 30 to 60 seconds. Add more water if the dough is too dry, in 1/2 Tablespoon increments.

Change out the flat beater for the dough hook. Turn to speed 2 and knead for 2 minutes. Remove the dough and knead by hand for 2 minutes. Let it rest for 20 to 30 minutes.

Cut dough into four pieces before processing with pasta sheet attachment. Take one piece and flatten into a rectangular shape. Adding flour to both sides. Be sure to cover the other pieces. Attach the pasta sheet roller to your stand mixer and set it to #1. Turn on the stand mixer to speed 2 and run the pasta dough through the pasta sheet roller. While on #1, fold the dough in half and run it through again. I do this several times.

Adding a little bit of flour on each side of the dough again, change setting to #2 and pass the pasta dough through the sheet roller. I do this twice and then twice each on #3 and then #4. If you want thicker dough, don't do the #4 setting.

Once again, add flour to each side of your long pasta sheet. Change the attachment to your spaghetti or fettuccine cutter and turn on to speed 2. Run the pasta sheet through and with your left hand, hold on to the pasta as it comes through the cutter. It's usually really long so I cut it and then wind it around my hand to create a nest. Allow pasta to dry for a few minutes before boiling.

When boiling your pasta, it only needs 3 to 7 minutes to boil.

With this pasta recipe, I prefer the fettuccine cutter.

Red Oil Wonton

Szechuan style red oil wonton with unique Sichuan style red oil, black vinegar, soy sauce and sesame oil.

2 Servings

30 wonton wrappers	**2 tablespoons black vinegar**
1 cup minced pork	**1 tablespoon sesame oil**
Pinch of salt	**2 tablespoon cooking wine**
1 tablespoon minced ginger	**½ teaspoon sugar**
1 tablespoon minced green onion	**pinch of salt**
1 small size egg	**1 tablespoon light soy sauce**
1 tablespoon oyster sauce	**2 garlic cloves, smashed**
Red oil dressing	**½ tablespoon minced green onion**
3-6 tablespoons Szechuan style chili oil, depends how spicy you want	**Minced coriander**
	1 cup water from cooking wonton

Preparation

You'd better to prepare the chili oil in the previous day according to this instruction.

Making red oil wonton

In a large bowl, mix minced pork with ginger, oyster sauce, egg, spring onion and salt. Keep stirring the mixture in one direction until well combined and sticky.

Refrigerate for around 15 minutes for a better flavor.

Assemble wonton one by one.

In a bowl, mix all the seasonings together.

Cook wonton in boiling water for 3 to 4 minutes until the wrappers become transparent completely. You can add some green vegetable like lettuce, bok choy leaves in last minute. Transfer out to serving bowl and then scoop some water to cover most of the wontons (not too much as it may dilute the red oil dressing).

Pour the red oil dressing on top; garnish extra minced spring onion and coriander. Mix well before enjoying.

Shredded Barbecue Chicken

Prep Time: 20 mins Cook Time: 25 mins

Makes 6 servings

1 pound boneless skinless chicken breasts

1/4 teaspoon pepper

1 can (14-1/2 ounces) reduced-sodium chicken broth, divided

1 cup hickory smoke-flavored barbecue sauce

1/4 cup molasses

1 tablespoon ground ancho chile pepper

1/2 teaspoon ground cinnamon

2-1/4 cups water

1 cup quick-cooking grits

1 cup canned pumpkin

3/4 cup shredded pepper jack cheese

1 medium tomato, seeded and chopped

6 tablespoons reduced-fat sour cream

2 green onions, chopped

2 tablespoons minced fresh cilantro

Preparation

Sprinkle chicken with pepper; place in a large nonstick skillet.

In a large bowl, combine 1 cup broth, barbecue sauce, molasses, chile pepper and cinnamon; pour over chicken. Bring to a boil. Reduce heat; cover and simmer until a thermometer inserted in chicken reads 165°, 20-25 minutes. Shred meat with 2 forks and return to the skillet.

Meanwhile, in a large saucepan, bring water and remaining broth to a boil. Slowly stir in grits and pumpkin. Reduce heat; cook and stir until thickened, 5-7 minutes. Stir in cheese until melted.

Divide grits among 6 serving bowls; top each with 1/2 cup chicken mixture. Serve with tomato, sour cream, green onions and cilantro.

Guacamole

Total Time

Prep: 15 min. + chilling

Makes 2-1/2 cups

3 medium ripe avocados, peeled and pitted

1/3 cup chopped sweet onion

1 small tomato, seeded and chopped

1 celery rib, finely chopped

2 garlic cloves, minced

2 tablespoons lemon or lime juice

2 teaspoons Worcestershire sauce

1/2 teaspoon salt

1/4 teaspoon pepper

1/4 to 1/3 cup chopped fresh cilantro, optional

Tortilla chips

Preparation

In a small bowl, mash avocados. Stir in onion, tomato, celery, garlic, lemon juice, Worcestershire, salt, pepper and, if desired, cilantro. Chill 1 hour before serving. Serve with chips.

Pulled Pork

Prep: 20 min. Cook: 8-1/2 hours

12 servings

1 boneless pork shoulder butt roast (3 to 4 pounds)

1 can (12 ounces) root beer or cola

1 bottle (18 ounces) barbecue sauce

12 kaiser rolls, split

Preparation

Place roast in a 4- or 5-qt. slow cooker. Add root beer; cook, covered, on low until meat is tender, 8-10 hours.

Remove roast; cool slightly. Discard cooking juices. Shred pork with two forks; return to slow cooker. Stir in barbecue sauce. Cook, covered, until heated through, about 30 minutes. Serve on rolls.

About the Author

Natasha Miller is a seasoned nutritionist and dieting expert with over a decade of experience in the health and wellness industry. Driven by her love of food and her passion for helping others, Melody has helped hundreds of clients transform their wellbeing through dietary changes and wellness coaching.